T0330118

Collaborative Inquiry for Organization Development and Change

Rami – to Mia, Eli, Eva and Levi that kept Elaine and me going during the COVID-19 pandemic home bound endeavor
and
David – to his friend and colleague, David Tuohy, whose untimely death from cancer shortly before the outbreak of the COVID-19 pandemic deprived him of a treasured friendship and valued intellectual support and challenge

Collaborative Inquiry for Organization Development and Change

Abraham B. (Rami) Shani

Professor of Management, Orfalea College of Business, California Polytechnic State University, USA

David Coghlan

Professor Emeritus, Trinity Business School, Trinity College Dublin, Ireland

 Edward Elgar
PUBLISHING

Cheltenham, UK • Northampton, MA, USA

Published by
Edward Elgar Publishing Limited
The Lypiatts
15 Lansdown Road
Cheltenham
Glos GL50 2JA
UK

Edward Elgar Publishing, Inc.
William Pratt House
9 Dewey Court
Northampton
Massachusetts 01060
USA

A catalogue record for this book
is available from the British Library

Library of Congress Control Number: 2020952077

This book is available electronically in the **Elgar**online
Business subject collection
http://dx.doi.org/10.4337/9781800378254

ISBN 978 1 80037 824 7 (cased)
ISBN 978 1 80037 825 4 (eBook)

Printed and bound by CPI Group (UK) Ltd, Croydon, CR0 4YY

'As scientists, we ask ourselves how we can contribute more to the amelioration of the most challenging issues of our time, such as global pandemics, climate change, social justice. Too frequently, hard science is ignored by leaders and policy makers. Shani and Coghlan help us understand that there is a better way for science to influence decision makers. Instead of lengthy papers explaining our findings, taking a collaborative inquiry approach of working with leaders to fashion scientifically-supported solutions is a more promising pathway. Collaborative inquiry is built to provide a scientific approach to change and Shani and Coghlan have been the masters of that approach for decades. This new book should be read by any scientist or leader who wants to make progress instead of just bemoaning the current state of affairs.'
Professor William A. (Bill) Pasmore, Professor of Practice, Teachers College, Columbia University, USA.

'This book is one of the best exemplars of showing how these two practices – research and helping – can inform each other constructively. This book is a welcome exploration of how these practices have enlarged our understanding of how human systems really work, how they must be studied, and how we can constructively intervene in them.'
Edgar H. Schein, Professor Emeritus, The Sloan School of Management, MIT, Co-author of *Humble Consulting*.

'In a world where organizations are facing unprecedented and increasingly complex challenges management scholars should have an important role to play. Unfortunately, they all too seldom do. In this context, "Collaborative Inquiry for Organization Development and Change", Shani and Coghlan make an important contribution by offering an inspiring perspective and tool box for how managers and researchers may engage in the joint construction of knowledge – to the benefit of both practice and research.'
Professor Andreas Werr, Stockholm School of Economics, Sweden.

Contents

List of figures		viii
List of tables		ix
About the authors		x
Foreword 1 – Massimo S. Brunelli		xii
Foreword 2 – Michael Beer		xvi
Preface		xix
1	Introducing collaborative inquiry	1
2	Theoretical foundations	17
3	Methodology and methods of inquiry	36
4	Transformation and design	52
5	Phases, mechanisms and quality	67
6	The researcher, theorizing and opportunities	86
Epilogue		95
Afterword – Philip H. Mirvis		98
References		105
Index		117

Figures

1.1	The core elements of collaborative inquiry	5
2.1	The theoretical foundations of collaborative inquiry	18
3.1	Methodology and methods of collaborative inquiry	37
3.2	The dynamics of enacting collaborative inquiry	45
4.1	Collaborative inquiry: transformation and design	53
4.2	Organizational transformation orientation: institutionalizing and activation forces	56
4.3	Directiveness and structuring	61
5.1	Phases in collaborative inquiry	70
5.2	Quality dimensions of collaborative inquiry	82
E.1	Collaborative inquiry as an olive tree	96

Tables

2.1	Modes 1 and 2 knowledge production	32
3.1	The structure of human knowing and doing	43
5.1	Collaborative inquiry: phases, practices and activities	79
5.2	Ensuring the quality dimensions of collaborative inquiry	84

About the authors

Abraham B. (Rami) Shani is Professor of Management at the Orfalea College of Business, California Polytechnic State University, California, USA. He holds a doctorate from Case Western Reserve University, Cleveland, Ohio, USA. Rami served as a Chair of the Organization Development and Change Division, Academy of Management. He has authored, co-authored or co-edited numerous books and research volumes. Rami has worked with many companies around the globe and diverse industries on issues that centered on creativity & innovation, new product development, organization design and development, change strategy and sustainability. He has published over 200 articles and book chapters. His most recent book (co-authored with David Coghlan) is *Conducting Action Research* (SAGE, 2018). He co-edited (with David Coghlan) four volumes of *Fundamentals of Organization Development* (SAGE, 2010) and *Action Research in Business and Management* (SAGE, 2016). Rami also co-edited *The Handbook of Collaborative Management Research* (SAGE, 2008), since 2008 is the co-editor of the annual research series, *Research in Organization Change and Development* (Emerald Publications) and is on the editorial board of five journals.

David Coghlan is Professor Emeritus at the Trinity Business School, University of Dublin Trinity College, Ireland and is a Fellow Emeritus of the College. He specializes in organization development and action research and participates actively in both communities internationally. He has published over 200 articles and book chapters. Recent books include: *Doing Action Research in Your Own Organization* (5th edn. SAGE, 2019), *Conducting Action Research for Business and Management Students* (with Rami Shani, SAGE, 2018) and *Inside Organizations* (SAGE, 2016). He is co-editor (with Mary Brydon-Miller) of the *SAGE Encyclopedia of Action Research* and with Rami Shani of the four-volume sets, *Fundamentals of Organization Development* (SAGE, 2010) and *Action Research in Business and Management* (SAGE, 2016). He is a member of the editorial advisory board of several journals, including *Action Research, The Journal of Applied Behavioral Science, Action Learning: Research and Practice, Systemic Practice and Action Research* and *OD Review*.

Foreword 1

Massimo S. Brunelli[1]

I am well aware of the line of research that goes by the name of collaborative inquiry. I share its epistemological approach and practical utility, having collaborated with one of the scholars who co-authored this book in two companies of which I have been and was the CEO during the research. As part of the managerial profession, it should be natural to feel the need to carry out one's own business with great openness towards the experience of others, drawing the most appropriate suggestions from scientific research to identify which are the best tools to face and solve problems at the company where you work.

Just as a doctor must necessarily know the research and studies that are published in his field, in order to have the most advanced medical-surgical, diagnostic and pharmacological techniques, a manager should do the same. But the analogy ends here. In fact, managers often do not feel they have to continue studying to do their job better. Often, especially those who have always dedicated their professional lives to the same sector do not believe that there is much new to learn in light of the experience they have accumulated.

In partial exculpation of the managerial profession, it must be said that frequently, however, managers do not find the tools and approach they need in academic research. In fact, in the context of business economics studies, it is very easy to remain frustrated with how little they can be used in the daily life of a manager.

In my experience I have encountered disciplines, such as corporate finance or accounting, where the manager is given positive knowledge, that is, a series of elements and tools with which to face problems and decide what to do; in other cases this seems more rare to me – I refer to disciplines such as strategy or business organization or change management. In these fields of study, the nature of research is mainly taxonomic: it classifies and organizes the possible situations that a manager is facing, but very often it does not tell her what she should do. Unfortunately, there are many studies that belong to this category; very useful for accumulating academic publications, but irrelevant to those who run a company and, above all, responsible for a furrow between academia and managerial profession which still seems to me very broad.

We know very well that the life of an organization does not have the determinism on which scientific disciplines can rely. But this does not exempt us from finding a method to be able, however, to define a set of knowledge that allows us to identify which is the best way for a given company to make strategic decisions, to define its organization or effectively measure its performance.

The instrument of collaborative inquiry goes precisely in this direction. It is an approach in which the scholar, aware of the problems that managers and operators daily experience in the field, sets up a collaborative study of these needs through engagement and active involvement of organization members and collaborative interaction with management. In such an effort, the organization is invited to participate in the framing and re-framing of the study, its methodology, data collection and data interpretation. Using tools like questionnaires and direct interviews it discusses and analyzes the results of these surveys with those directly involved, thus initiating conversations with organization members about what the data means. The study teams collected the data and interpreted the data following basic scientific rigor. It is therefore a setting that can also allow academic research to move in the right direction and generate useful and relevant knowledge. I have had direct experience of it.

I met the colleagues from the Polytechnic de Milano and California Polytechnic State University for the first time as part of a project on creativity, which is of fundamental importance for a company like the one I was managing at the time, that is, a fashion design and textile company. Understanding our business and our know-how about creativity was an important step forward. We all spoke of creativity as an essential quality of our work, only to find out that this concept within our organization did not always have the same meaning. Here is a fundamental result of the work inspired by the collaborative inquiry project. It allowed us to get to use the same language, leaving behind the babble that is often the source of endless discussions and few concrete actions in companies. Let us always remember – the biblical passage teaches us – that nothing is more complicated to manage than an organization where the same language is not spoken. From there we went ahead and understood what the best conditions were to create a habitat in the company that was conducive to the development of professional ideas and practices which could direct creative talent towards creative collectives that translated into economically and commercially appreciable results.

I resumed the collaboration with the external researchers a couple of years later. We returned to work together on a different project in the context of a different company – a company operating in the real estate funds sector, born two years earlier from a merger between two competing companies, one based in Rome and the other in Milan. This was, in effect, a new company, formed from the two very different companies from which it originated, looking for its identity. Inspired by collaborative inquiry process we realized that the main challenge for enhancing our success had to do with multiple and distinct mini subcultures. We moved forward to develop a "common culture" and engaged most of the members of the organization in crafting the "ideal culture."

Our study team, after careful examinations of the scholarly literature recommended to follow the Cameron and Quinn model proposed in their book, *Diagnosis and Changing Organizational Cultures* (2011) and – incredible but true – we applied it to the concrete case of our company. We were thus able to understand what our managers' and employees' perceptions of the corporate culture was, discovering that we thought we were a company focused on stability and control, built on procedural and organizational rigor to be a market leader. From the work done internally and always guided and inspired by external researchers, we came to realize that we would like to be more flexible in our approach to organization and the market. From these results we began to understand what we wanted to be. It is the next phase of the research which will lead us to analyze the gap between what we are and what we should be. Above all, we intend to identify what actions to take to bridge this gap. We have therefore identified nine phases of a work program, which moves towards the things to do: from the so-called small wins, which allow rapid changes, to the agenda in terms of leadership style and communication strategy.

To conclude, the strength of the approach presented in this book is that it goes beyond empirical research alone, that is, the collection of data or the examination of business cases. Thanks to the direct and interactive exchange and collaboration of company members and externally, through honest collaboration, while following rigorous analysis methods, the practice of collaborative inquiry manages to combine the strength of academic deduction with that of induction of managerial practice.

In other words, thanks to it, my colleagues and I have managed to do our job better.

NOTE

1. Massimo Brunelli has served as a CEO of Mantero and IdeaFimit. This foreword was written for a book, *Collaborative Management Research: Teoria, Methodi, Esperienze* (Milan: Raffaello Cortina, 2014). We are grateful to Raffaello Cortina for permission to publish this translation here.

Foreword 2

Michael Beer[1]

A discouraging seventy percent of corporate transformations don't live up to expectations. Many managers I have spoken to think their own company simply cannot change, much as it needs to. They've seen previous efforts fail and they have a pretty good idea why they failed. Since the underlying reasons for failure haven't changed, why should the results? But in a business environment demanding rapid adaptation to everything from ever changing competitive challenges to COVID to robots to Black Lives Matter, so much failure to transform is unacceptable. Indeed, this is reflected in the decreasing tenure of CEOs and the public's decreasing trust in institutions. A better way has to be found and this book makes an important contribution to our knowledge about how that can be done through collaborative inquiry and action.

My first consulting engagement was at a factory whose leadership wanted to become a "Theory Y" organization – Douglas McGregor's designation for participative management (McGregor, 1960). Naturally, I began with a workshop to teach them the *ideas* underlying Theory Y and participative management. Senior management told me this was interesting but not helpful. I then pivoted to working collaboratively with managers on solving their immediate problems. That led to new insights, confirmed by subsequent experience and field research, about the power of collaborative inquiry and conversation to develop better solutions. Better, in part, because the process of developing the solution simultaneously develops what's usually missing – commitment to that solution.

As the authors of this book show, abstract ideas generated by "normal" positivistic research do not help managers because they are uncontextualized; they do not reflect the specific and grounded circumstances of a particular organization as understood by its members. Moreover, knowledge-first approaches to change assume that re-education will transform attitudes and ultimately behavior. This assumption misses the point. Changes in behavior occur only when people are involved in identifying problems, diagnosing the causes, and then redesigning their organization and their own behavior and practices. Organizations are systems in which causality is both multifaceted and circular. That is, a multitude of hard (technical) and soft (social and emotional) facets are always at work and are always affecting each other. Thus, for valid solutions and commitment to be developed, those within the system must be involved, especially those at the top who will have to lead and manage differently.

In a study of corporate transformation, my colleagues and I found that change programs launched from the top – usually consisting of education and training but sometimes also involving changes in structure, policies, and practices – failed to change much (Beer et al., 1990). Pressure for short-term results and the leaders' natural desire to avoid the topic of their own ineffectiveness blinded them to the need for a slower – potentially more painful – collaborative process of discovery, learning and change. Meanwhile, the lower levels, who, I have found, know a lot about why the organization is not working, are unable to speak truth to power about barriers to effectiveness, trust and commitment. As Chris Argyris noted, hierarchical organizations – that's *all* organizations – are built for cover-up.

No abstract journal article or education program can overcome these realities. An experience I had while teaching in the Harvard Business School's Advanced Management Program confirms this. Toward the end of the program participants – all senior executives in their company – asked to speak with me. They thought my ideas about organizational effectiveness and change were important and relevant to their own organization, but they were sure that their CEO and their senior team did not and would not understand the problems they themselves now recognized. They saw their organization's system of organizing, managing and leading stuck in neutral and even though they now felt they knew what needed to be done, they didn't see any way to convince their top management to act. As I myself have seen over and over, very many executives and managers feel trapped this way – and they might be surprised at how often their CEOs and senior teams feel similarly trapped. As the authors of this book argue, the only way out of this trap is a collaborative inquiry between those at the top and those below whose daily frustrations with the organization's ineffectiveness can provide those at the top with important insights into the problems that must be confronted and solved. Collaboration requires a partnership, open and honest conversations between the top team and key lower-level managers below them who know first hand and in detail what is working and not working. This honest conversation in turn requires a container – that is, a structure and process – that keeps it safe and productive so that it will lead to a different understanding of the system of organizing, managing and leading.

My own experience and research confirm that honest conversations consistently identify the organization's people as a strength, but also identify silent (that is, not openly discussable) barriers that frustrate people's efforts to execute senior management's strategic and values directions. These barriers are lack of clarity about strategy and values, poor coordination and collaboration attributable to a poorly designed organization by an ineffective leader and leadership team, inadequate leadership development and, consequently, a paucity of effective down-the-line leaders, and poor vertical communication and collaboration between the top and lower levels, particularly the inability of lower levels to speak truth to power. That prevents the requisite open and honest collaborative inquiry required for productive change. These barriers are difficult to talk about and therefore require an organization development consultant who facilitates the collaborative inquiry and offers managers valid heuristic frameworks with which to redesign their system of organizing, managing and leading. Nevertheless, it is the managers, not the consultant, who must decide and thereby arrive at the commitment needed to transform the system. The most important lesson here for managers is the collaborative inquiry process itself. The process must be safe for those involved, and have no negative consequences for the people involved. If the collaborative inquiry is successful, the organization may choose to use it repeatedly as its method of change and its engine of continuous learning, improvement and development. That is what it will take to survive and prosper.

NOTE

1.   Harvard Business School and Center for Higher Ambition Leadership.

Preface

We started this endeavor knowing that we wanted to capture some of the organization development and change research in which we have been engaging over the past few decades and to offer it to scholar-practitioners as an approach to making a difference in organizations and generating practical knowledge. We have worked together on different projects over 20 years. In undertaking this journey, we discovered that true collaborative work, while living on two continents, is doable and can be successful. The restrictions imposed by the COVID-19 pandemic enabled us to devote ourselves full-time to this collaborative venture. With an eight-hour time difference, continuous cycles of drafts and redrafts and daily Skype check-ins and reviews allowed us to have intense work schedules over the five months. Such a collaborative venture requires continuous dialogue, open and honest conversations, humble inquiry and willingness to work through differences. By the end of this endeavor, while the quality of our relationship is at a much higher level (and so is the trust level), we appreciate even more the fact that we do have distinct mindsets and do still see the world somewhat differently. In many ways, the emerging process of developing this book resembles the collaborative inquiry process advanced in this volume.

Both of us are deeply appreciative of our respective mentors who formed us in the collaborative way of understanding and conducting research that is counter-cultural in the contemporary business and management school academy. Rami acknowledges his debt to Bill Pasmore, David Brown, David Kolb and Frank Friedlander, who taught him about the value of emergent change and development processes, the importance of guiding conceptual framework, the role of mindset and the quality of relationship in inquiring into and with a living system. Rami also would like to acknowledge his appreciation for the Innovation and Design as Leadership (IDeaLs) collaborative research community – Roberto Verganti, Joseph Press, Tommaso Buganza, Paola Bellis, Daniel Trabucchi, Silvia Maganimi and Federico Zasa and the seven companies' partners – for bringing collaborative inquiry to the forefront of collaboration-in-action. David acknowledges his debt to Ed Schein, who taught him the values of process, interiority, practical knowing and inquiring in the present tense in a mode of humble inquiry. We thank Mike Beer and Phil Mirvis for their support and encouragement in the Foreword and Afterword, respectively. We are deeply appreciative of the work of Lexie Conat, who skillfully transformed our crude drawings into sophisticated diagrams, and to Jayne Behman for putting a visual expression on our generative image. We thank the Edward Elgar team, Francine O'Sullivan and Natasha Rozenberg, freelance copyeditor Brian North, and freelance proofreader Fern Labram.

1. Introducing collaborative inquiry

The context within which organizations function is continuously changing. The rate of change is faster than ever. An acronym that expresses
this context is VUCA (volatile, uncertain, complex, ambiguous). In
coping with and adapting to the VUCA world a wide variety of types of
changes are required and need to be implemented in order to survive and
to grow. Changes lie in the area of technology (McGrath & McManus,
2020), innovation (Verganti, 2017), work practices (Pasmore, 2015),
how organizations are designed (Beer, 2020) and the nature of workplace spaces (Spreitzer et al., 2020). The amount of change creates
opportunities to develop greater understanding of the new business and
organizational potential. The above suggests that the most critical need
today is to develop the capacity to change continuously (Pasmore, 2020).
A collaborative inquiry orientation builds on the heritage and achieve-
ments in the field of organization development and change, and provides
a comprehensive approach for continuously addressing the needs of the
emerging new workplace.

A central dilemma for executives and leaders is how to sustain what
work, how to trigger innovations to address the changing market, how
to lead the transformation, and how to build the capacity for continuous
learning practice. A wide variety of mental models and guiding road
maps has evolved over the last 70 years in the field of organization
development and change. A review of the different categorization and
clustering of organization development and change interventions is
beyond the scope of this book. Collaborative inquiry is grounded in
a process-oriented practice that is coupled with inquiry in the present
tense, humble inquiry and engaged scholarship.

An additional context that underpins collaborative inquiry is a changing understanding of the nature of organizational research. A significant
foundation on which collaborative inquiry organization development is
built is the philosophy of knowledge creation known as Mode 2 knowledge production. Gibbons et al. (1994) distinguished between Mode 1
and Mode 2 knowledge production approaches in their book, *The New
Production of Knowledge* and subsequent writings (Gibbons et al., 2011;

Nowotny et al., 2001, 2003). They describe Mode 1 research as characterized by the explanatory knowledge that is generated in a disciplinary context, which arises from the academic agenda, and describe the role of the researcher as an observer with a detached and neutral relationship to the setting. The type of knowledge acquired is universal knowledge in that the data are context free and validated by logic, measurement, and consistency of prediction and control. In most respects Mode 1 captures the normal meaning of the term "science." In contrast, Gibbons and colleagues present Mode 2 as the new knowledge production where knowledge is created in the context of application and is transdisciplinary. In Chapter 2 we will elaborate on the key features of Mode 2 orientation in terms of the theoretical foundation of collaborative inquiry and organization development and change.

Mindset, or interpretive schemas, play a critical role in the way managers and scholars address the growing challenges of continuous change, transformation, organization development, inquiry and collaboration. Mindset is broadly viewed as a set of assumptions, ways of thinking and behaving held by individuals and social systems about humans, organizations, society, change and growth. Within the context of this book, our focus is on the mindset or interpretive schemas held by individuals and groups about collaborative inquiry as a way to engage and impact organization change and development. Mindset impacts a person's and social system's ability to create meaning of a specific business situation and dynamics. The meaning-making process – both at the individual and group level – will impact the quality of actions taken based on new discoveries. Transforming individuals' mindset and creating a collective mindset is viewed as an integral part of the collaborative inquiry process.

DEFINITION AND CORE ELEMENTS OF COLLABORATIVE INQUIRY

Collaborative inquiry involves partnership, engaged scholarship and humble inquiry in the process of organization development and change initiatives. The terms collaborative, inquiry, partnership, engaged scholarship, humble inquiry, cooperative venture, shared power and engaging in different forms of knowing are central to describing and guiding organization development and change work. In this opening chapter we introduce the broad framework and some of the fundamentals of collaborative inquiry for organization development and change. Building on the tradition of organization development and change field, our notion of collaborative inquiry is grounded in conversation or dialogue that occurs within a partnership or cooperative venture between those who are insiders to the organization and outside researchers based on shared power with the aim of both addressing relevant organizational issues and creating practical knowledge about organizational change. Such an endeavor occurs through the partnership and through a dialogical process by creating generative images and shared meaning. It takes place in the present tense, draws on different mode of knowing, and the role of the scholar-practitioner is that of an engaged partner enacting humble inquiry.

We define collaborative inquiry (CI) as a dialogic emergent inquiry process between two or more parties, at least one of whom is a member of the system/organization/network and at least one of whom is an external consultant/researcher, for the dual purpose of taking actions and creating new and shared meaning in order to improve and/or develop a system and of generating new understanding of an issue or phenomenon. It is simultaneously concerned with developing new partnerships based on a knowledge or expertise as opposed to power based on position or role and bringing about change in systems. It focuses on developing a system's self-help competencies through mastering the process of generative image creation and collective sense-making/meaning-making. It creates social space for dialogue that enables individuals to think, feel and act outside of the organizational hierarchy, rules, norms, imagery and language. It enhances the development of individuals and collective mindsets or interpretive schemas. It provides new organizational capabilities to aid system transformation. Finally, it takes place in the present tense and is therefore an emergent change process within a complex adaptive system that aims at developing a genuine partnership in the process of change and new knowledge creation.

The key elements of collaborative inquiry in this definition are: (i) how it is grounded in partnership, conversation or dialogue between those who are insiders to the organization and researchers who are outsiders; (ii) how its aim is to both address relevant organizational issues and to create practical knowledge about organizational change though the partnership and through a dialogical process by creating generative images and shared understanding; (iii) how it is a cooperative venture within a newly created social space where the dynamics are between equals in non-hierarchical relationships that are based on expertise; and (iv) how it is embedded in the present-tense emergent process.

The dynamic nature of the business environment – its context – suggest that most changes are triggered by outside forces (i.e., technological development, societal priorities, legislation, worldwide competition), many of whom the organization have little control over or at best little ability to influence. Hence the VUCA acronym. We view organizations as complex adaptive sociotechnical systems. What we mean is that organizations comprise both a technical system and a social or people system which are interdependent and which are constantly adapting to the changing context. Figure 1.1 captures the working framework of collaborative inquiry for organization development and change. The core elements are: (i) the view of organizations as socially adaptive learning entities; (ii) how its aim is to address a relevant organizational issue and to generate new knowledge; (iii) drawing on a wide knowledge-base of the field of organization development and change; (iv) building on Mode 2 knowledge production orientation; (v) utilizing engaged scholarship and humble inquiry orientation; and (vi) all embedded in honest partnership. The theoretical foundation will be explored in more detail in Chapter 2.

ORGANIZATIONS AS COMPLEX, ADAPTIVE SOCIALLY CONSTRUCTED SYSTEMS

Organizations are viewed as complex social entities that function within a highly interdependent world and complex local ecosystem. Complex adaptive systems are composed of many interactive agents, each with its own strategy for adapting to the environment and pursuing its goals (Miller & Page, 2007). Following the foundational work of Bertalanffy (1950), Checkland (1981), Emery and Trist (1965) and Miller and Page (2007), we view organizations as complex adaptive sociotechnical systems composed of interacting humans, using knowledge, technology and tools to produce goods or services valued by customers.

Organizations are social constructions (Campbell, 2000). They are artifacts created by human beings to serve their ends. They follow processes that are shaped and affected by human purposes, values and intended outcomes and they do not exist independently of human minds and actions. They are, in effect, communities created by meaning, with a rich tapestry of cultural rules, roles and interactions. In other words, they are adaptive social spaces in which people share a common purpose and have a relationship with one another that frames a shared vision, organizes, decides strategies and plans, implements those strategies and

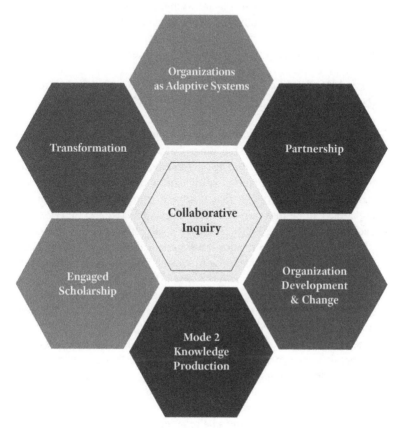

Figure 1.1   The core elements of collaborative inquiry

plans in cycles of adaption and coping in a VUCA world. Accordingly, exploring meanings and creating new meanings are central to collaborative inquiry.

Learning is an integral part of any living meaning-making system (March, 1991). As such, a myriad of organizational learning facets can be found in the organizational literature; for example, learning as an individual or as a group; organizational, inter-organizational, network and work-based phenomenon; and learning as knowledge acquisition, adaptation, skill learning and development of knowledge bases (Lipshitz et al., 2007; Coughlan & Coghlan, 2011). As social entities within a dynamic business context, organizations develop learning capabilities as a way to survive. Learning mechanisms usually emerge in a natural way and tend to be enhanced purposefully within an organization in order to ensure survival and enhance performance and innovation (Shani & Docherty 2003). We will develop this foundation in Chapter 2.

COLLABORATIVE INQUIRY AND ORGANIZATION DEVELOPMENT AND CHANGE

The social science of organization development and change (ODC) is viewed as engaging with the meanings that people attribute to and create in their activities of envisioning, organizing, strategizing, acting and evaluating and creating practical knowledge about organizational change (Coghlan et al., 2019). The rich history of organization development and change can be traced to the work of Lewin, Trist and Emery seven decades ago (Pasmore, 2001; Bradbury et al., 2008; Burnes & Cooke, 2012). The routes of organization development and change are embedded in process of helping organizations to survive, develop and prosper while adhering to a humanistic value set (Neilsen, 1984). Schein (1969) argued that working with organizations requires a deep insight into work and organizing processes. He further advocates that at the roots of ODC one can find process-oriented practice (Schein, 2010). Collaborative inquiry focuses on the process of engaging and enabling the conversations that organizational members need to hold among themselves about the current challenges, opportunities and activities in order that they may explore new meaning of their experience, their understanding and guide actions. This was expressed by Schein as process consultation which he defined as a consultant creating a helping relationship with a client which enables the client 'to perceive, understand and act on the process events that occur in the client's internal and external environment in order to improve the situation as defined by the client' (Schein, 1999: 20).

PARTNERSHIP AND COLLABORATIVE INQUIRY

At the center of collaborative inquiry is the drive to initiate and develop authentic partnerships between all those engaged in the effort. Partnership suggests joint ownership of the initiative in which each partner brings with them a specific set of supplementary skills, experience and knowledge. The cooperative venture between the individuals involved is based on equality. The relationships are viewed as non-hierarchical and are based on expertise and knowledge and not power driven by role function or position (Kraus, 1980). The quality of the relationship in the partnership is influenced by the nature of the context that resulted in the desire to form the partnership, the alignment of purpose between the partners, the degree of commitment to the initiative, and the degree of trust and openness to be influenced by the partner(s) (Huxham & Vangen, 2005). The quality of the partnership influences the ability to initiate and conduct honest dialogue (Beer, 2020; Schein, 2016). Partnerships develop and mature over time as the joint inquiry is carried out and as the relationships evolve. Over time partnerships tend to develop their own subcultures, common language, and work routines (Mohrman & Shani, 2008).

ADDRESSSING RELEVANT ISSUES AND KNOWLEDGE CREATION

Unlike laboratory studies in which situations are artificially created to study the relationships between independent variables, or survey inquiries that center on an attempt to understand a priori research question(s) that are developed in a detached process, collaborative inquiry takes place with and within a living system based on the desire or need to address an issue confronting the organization, whether strategic or operational. The focus of collaborative inquiry is to generate the practical knowledge that enables the organization to make relevant changes and to contribute actionable knowledge to the social science of organizational change and development. We will elaborate further on the philosophy of practical knowing in Chapter 2.

Another distinct feature of collaborative inquiry is the realization that inquiry takes place in the present tense (Coghlan & Shani, 2017). As organizational members and researchers conduct collaborative inquiry, they have to engage with issues that are present in the organization at that time and those issues that emerge during the inquiry. The dialogic and change processes typically throw up differences of understanding and differences in interpreting the meaning of events. A particular intervention may produce unexpected or undesired outcomes. Data shift as a consequence of discussions, decisions and actions. Participants have to work with data that emerge from the inquiry itself and which change as the process proceeds. This means that the participants have to be attentive to the emergent data, both in the substantive issues of the change and in the collaborative dynamics between the participants, and to inquire into them; in other words, to be inquiring in the present tense. We will elaborate further on inquiring in the present tense in Chapter 2.

In collaborative inquiry in organization development, the role of the ODC researcher is understood to be a facilitator of the creation and enactment of the social and psychological space whereby organizational members can converse about the organization and its future (Friedman et al., 2016). We understand this role in terms of engaged scholarship (Van de Ven, 2007) and humble inquiry (Schein, 2013, 2016). Engaged scholarship is broadly viewed as a participative form of research for generating action while obtaining the insights of those involved and incorporating the perspectives of key stakeholders (Van de Ven, 2011).

Schein (1969) originally framed his approach as process consultation which we have defined above as enabling the client to see what is happening and understand it so as to create action for change. Latterly, Schein has moved to emphasizing the disposition of being 'humble', which he defines as 'the fine art of drawing someone out, of asking questions to which you do not already know the answer, of building a relationship based on curiosity and interest in the other person' (2013: 2). What is also significant in this regard is the distinction between this model of helping and that more dominant doctor–patient model where experts are brought in to diagnose a problem and prescribe solutions. These notions of the engaged scholarship and humble inquiry underpin our understanding of the role of the ODC researcher in collaborative inquiry.

WAYS OF KNOWING IN COLLABORATIVE INQUIRY

The stereotypical view of the nature of knowing in research is that it is abstract, conceptual and theoretical in describing the relationship between pre-determined variables. Like all stereotypes there is a truth and a limitation to such a view. In the context of organizations as complex adaptive sociotechnical systems, collaborative inquiry engages with several forms of knowing, what Heron and Reason (1997) call an 'extended epistemology'. When researchers and organizational members engage in collaborative inquiry they utilize and seek to know in several modes of knowing. They examine technical issues in a scientific mode; they build a partnership relationship and work together in a relational mode; they may draw on creative imagery to express their sense of the present situation and their vision of the future in a presentational mode; and they work in a practical mode to change the organization. We will elaborate further on the different forms of knowing, especially that of practical knowing, in Chapter 2.

COLLABORATIVE INQUIRY, ACTION RESEARCH AND DIALOGIC ORGANIZATION DEVELOPMENT

As we frame the broad essence of collaborative inquiry it is important to place its theory and practice in the context of action research and dialogic organization development. These three terms coexist and overlap in many respects. Each aims at taking action and creating new insights of relevance, are viewed as an emergent endeavor, tend to emphasize the discovery and learning process, and pay attention to patterns and quality of relationships in the discovery process. At the most basic level, the three vary in terms of core value and areas of emphasis: Action research's primary focus is on taking action to address important social and organizational issues in collaboration with those directly affected by them and to cogenerate practical knowledge through the process. In doing so it utilizes a general empirical method through engaging individual reflection and collaborative action in the present tense through different forms of knowing (Coghlan, 2019). Dialogic organization development emphasizes the dialogic process, in contrast to a diagnostic one with the core emphasis on generative practice and insights (Bushe & Marshak, 2015). Collaborative inquiry emphasizes a structure of full partnership and engagement between a team of external researchers and insider organizational members in the co-design and implementation of the discovery process and organization transformation. In doing so it creates a system of equals – that is, based on expertise and not position power – in the search for new understanding and action. A comprehensive review of action research and dialogic organization development is beyond the scope of this book and is available in Coghlan (2019), Coghlan and Shani (2018) and Bushe and Marshak (2015).

VIGNETTE

Mia called her former professor a few years after graduating from an Executive MBA program. She recalled the course about organization development and change that she took with him as one of the most helpful courses in her program and wanted to meet for coffee and talk. Mia had worked in a company for the last seven years, was recently promoted to vice-president (VP) in a human resources (HR) position (she was one of five VPs and was the only woman in the executive suite). The company is in the agricultural machinery and tools-based industry. She had some ideas about a possible project. They agreed to meet the following week.

The company is a global concern located in the Mid-West USA and one of the top ten companies in its industry. The company specialized in the design, development and manufacturing of agricultural machinery and tools, such as tractors with all the necessary equipment for working out the land that can be modified to address the different needs of a wide variety of crops. Customers were loyal to the company based on product quality and a long tradition. Increased industry competitiveness was driven by a continuous development of advanced and digital technology.

During the conversation, Mia's major concern was that the company was not changing fast enough and feared that unless it developed its internal change capabilities it would have a hard time meeting goals and even surviving. She stated that while the chief executive officer (CEO) shared her concern, not all members of the executive team did. Mia thought that, based on the company's culture and history, a collaborative inquiry approach to learning and experimentation with alternative ways of thinking and working could work well.

Following a couple of meetings with the CEO and conversations with each of the VPs, a mutual decision was arrived at to launch a project. An external research team, comprising two senior and two junior researchers was engaged. The initial framing of the project was to understand the firm's current change capabilities with the intention of enhancing what works and develop new capabilities as needed. The project scope was presented to the executive team by the CEO in the presence of two members of the research team. Conversations about current and future challenges that the company faced were followed by the development of a shared definition of project scope, estimated timeline, resources and mechanisms. This conversation included articulating some ethical ground rules governing the use of information, for example ensuring anonymity and confidentiality and that information would not be used to the detriment of individuals. It was agreed that a three-member steering committee would be created (to be headed by the VP of HR and composed of one highly regarded division head and one highly respected research and development (R&D) team leader) and a cross-sectional study team (which would be a microcosm of the organization to the extent possible and be created by the steering committee in consultation with the executive committee) to carry out the initial phase of the study. The external researchers would be full partners. It was also agreed that for the first couple of phases of the study, the steering committee would meet once a week while the study team would meet two or three times a week as needed. The VP for HR would update the executive committee periodically about the study and its progress and solicit its input. The CEO communicated the study and its purpose to all members of the organization.

Following the formation of the steering committee and the nine-member study team, the study was launched. During the launch meeting the notion of cooperative endeavor among equals (while working on the study tasks) was emphasized. During a two-month period, the study team led an analysis of the company, its performance, its practices, what was understood to be its culture, and an initial exploration of the current adaptation or change capabilities. During this phase, the study team decided that interviews conducted by the external research team would be the most appropriate approach. The study team crafted the interview questions and interview protocol. Thirty members of the organization (who were selected using a stratified random sample technique) were interviewed by members of the external research team in sessions that each lasted 30 minutes. The raw data was compiled and clustered, based on an initial content analysis by the external research team, while protecting anonymity. The 20-page document of clustered raw data was shared with the study team for the purpose of data interpretation and sense-making. The preliminary shared understanding of the current state was reviewed and discussed with the steering committee and with the executive team such that further shared understanding and insights could be developed.

The researchers shared some relevant theory about capability and change capability. A capability is viewed as the capacity to undertake particular activities successfully in order to effect a desired end (Grant, 1996). Organization capabilities are viewed as composite bundles of competences, skills and technologies, rather than single discrete skills (Mohrman et al., 2006). Development of new capabilities entails the ability to integrate, build and configure internal and external competencies (skills, processes and structures) to address a rapidly changing environment (Teece, 2007; Teece et al., 1997). Change and development capabilities entail the ability to enhance and develop mechanisms that can aid the development of bundles of competences and learning mechanisms needed to continuously adapt to changing environmental business contexts. The researchers then led a conversation on how the theory on capabilities might inform the questions arising from the report from the interviews. The conceptual input and conversation provided the context for the next phase of the dialogue.

The steering committee, the study team and the research team began a series of conversations about the meaning of continuous change and change capabilities in the specific context of the company. The research question was reframed to be "What are the current change capabilities that the company needs to keep, what needs to be dropped, and what new capabilities need be developed and how might they be implemented?"

Following meetings between members of the executive committee, steering committee and study team members, the direction, approach and study mechanisms were laid out. Important to note is that during the meetings with the executive committee two of the VPs expressed doubt about the importance of the emerging focus and the need to prioritize it. Both expressed opinions that from where they sat, a more beneficial focus should be on the current company structure. They felt that the current structure was an "old" structure and required a re-visit. After some more discussion, the CEO concluded that for the long run, the focus needed to be on change capabilities, and if, during the study, the structure would be identified as a hindrance it would be addressed. The study team was split into two sub-teams; one would focus on systematic mapping and assessing of the current change capabilities and the other would focus on the exploration of possible change capabilities. It was agreed that both sub-teams would also have periodic meetings to share progress and insights. Each sub-team was enlarged to seven team members and each team was given the freedom to develop the most appropriate research methodology. Each team also included two members of the external research team.

The study team that focused on "mapping the current change capabilities" explored different research methodologies and decided to utilize a descriptive case study research design and methodology. They agreed to start with in-depth interviews with individuals that had led past changes in the company. The interviewees were invited to list past change initiatives that were implemented in the company over the previous decade, focus on one or two that they viewed as most impactful, and reflect on who had been involved, what their impact was, what made them successful, how success was measured, what the necessary capabilities were to design and lead the change, and so on. The interviewees were asked to come up with a phrase that captured recent changes in which they had been involved and draw a flowchart or a picture or an image of one or two change initiatives. Some drew a flowchart of the change process; some drew sketches that were abstracts. Some were more nature-related; a couple drew a winter storm; some drew white water; some drew a team hiking up a mountain with obstacles in their way; some drew a detailed happy face; some drew a quilt; and others drew cracked earth.

Twenty individuals were interviewed and the interviews lasted between 90 and 120 minutes. Following an analysis of the data by the study team, 25 change capabilities were identified as critical. The team developed a short survey that was distributed throughout the organization in which members were asked to respond to three issues: (1) The extent to which the organization displayed each change capability; (2) Rank order 25 change capabilities from the most to the least critical, and (3) What change capabilities should be eliminated and which ones should be enhanced. The methodology chosen (i.e., the instruments design, the data collection and data interpretation) were the results of ongoing conversations and collaboration between members of the study team, steering committee and executive team.

The study team that focused on the exploration of possible new change capabilities explored different research methodologies and decided to utilize design science research and methodology orientation. This orientation was chosen as the team agreed that it was critical to involve as many people in the process as they would be the ones to implement it. The team agreed that designing artifacts and making sense of them would trigger both creative idea generation and useful knowledge. The main steps that the team led included identification of the problem and the development of a few possible artifacts that could help address the problem. Each team member was asked to bring and share between three and five pictures that captured a new change capability. The sense-making of the different images created a different mental and social space that helped individuals to talk and reflect on how they were thinking about their organization in the future. Each team was asked to talk to three other members of the organization and ask them to bring up to three images that captured needed change capabilities for an informal conversation with the study team. Following the meetings, the study team had 40 different images and was challenged to create a collage that captured the essence of what was shared thus far. A graphic artist was hired to create a collage that encompassed what was shared. The artist came up with three different collages. The study team led meetings with both the steering committee and executive team to explore how they were making sense of the collages. The activities were powerful and a decision was made to give as many members of the organization as were interested an opportunity to take part in a broader collective sense-making activity.

Fifty individuals expressed interest in participating. Two sessions (of 90 minutes each, with 25 individuals) were organized and led by the study teams. Individuals were asked to write a story of what they saw, as it related to possible organization change capabilities, what it meant to them and what new ideas it generated. The narratives that were shared in the collective sense-making process were captured by the study team. The study sub-team, following the collective new meaning creation, compiled an initial list of the generated organizational change capabilities. A joint meeting of the two study sub-teams and steering committee focused on the development lists of specific skills, practices and processes: those that were perceived to have worked and which could be retained, those that needed to be eliminated, and those that needed to be developed. The essence of each item was briefly articulated and preliminary action steps were identified. Following a fishbowl design, the steering group and the study team met the executive committee to review and share their insights. Two of the executive team members were constantly critical of the project and expressed disagreement with every opinion and conclusion as the study team reviewed the suggestions and offered their conclusions. This was a serious challenge to the collaborative inquiry process, and the researchers realized that how they responded to the two executives in front of the others would be a critical test for the success of the partnership. As outsiders to the organization they were ignorant of any covert political agendas that might be at play, so they had to remain focused on the agenda while being attentive to the meeting's dynamics. Accordingly, they listened carefully, asked questions and worked to maintain a constructive conversation that focused on understanding of the ideas and what led to them.

The executive committee decided to adopt many of the ideas generated and came up with an action plan. The VPs were each charged to carry out the tasks that fell within their respective domains. The decision was made to phase out the change capabilities configurations that were not viewed as adding value within four weeks. Those that were to be kept and enhanced were to be reviewed within six weeks. Six individual champions were identified to lead the development of six new change capabilities: (1) generate specific ideas for a more agile company (change capability vision and strategy); (2) generate specific ideas and process for the development of more environmentally friendly products (environmental sustainability focus); (3) generate ideas for innovation and innovation leadership processes; (4) suggestions for a process for continuous improvement (and shortening) of the new product development process; (5) generate specific ideas for a process for continuous improvement of the manufacturing process, and (6) generate action steps to secure social sustainability (attracting and retaining human capital). Each champion had to present a possible mechanism, action plan and a process to carry out the task to the executive committee within four weeks. The study team was asked to continue to meet as needed and to serve as a resource and support for each of the champions. The steering committee would be phased out while two of the members (not including the HR VP) became a part of each of the study teams.

This project is still in progress as this chapter is being written. Beyond the relevant new insights generated thus far for the organization (such as the need to enhance the post-product development review process; structured periodic lunch meetings with "old" and "new" technology users for a dialogue about the product; creating a company/university office to enhance the relationship with university programs with internships and research support in the departments of mechanical engineering, robotics and crop science; revise the recruitment strategy and practice in order to attract new talent with capabilities that provide the foundation for emerging and future needs) several papers for academic journals and a book chapter are in advanced stage of development. Thus far, the joint outcomes for theory and practice are being met, while at the same time the collaborative inquiry efforts continue.

REFLECTION

This vignette provides a flavor of a collaborative inquiry initiative. The key elements of collaborative inquiry that we have introduced in this chapter are evident. The aim was to address the organizational issue of developing change capabilities and to create practical knowledge. The process was grounded in a partnership between the insider members of the organization and the external researchers. The partnership was enacted through the multiple conversations in which the researchers drew on their theoretical knowledge and the insiders on their practical knowledge from their experience. The researchers worked as engaged scholars, listening to the insiders' perspectives, questioning supportively, and actively helping the project develop. The process drew on different forms of knowing; for example, the narrative of organizational experiences, the codified analysis of the interviews, and the generative imagery of the collages. A developing relational knowing of building the partnership of trust, communication and shared dialogue was evident throughout the process. Evident, also, is the work in the present tense. As one meeting led to another and led to the project design and initial interviews which then led to the more extended interviews which led to the introduction of the artist and the collages, attentiveness to what was going on in the present tense was paramount. We will return to the vignette in later chapters.

CONCLUSIONS

In this opening chapter we have introduced the broad conceptual framework of collaborative inquiry in organization development and change. These fundamentals demonstrate how it is grounded in conversation or dialogue between those who are insiders to the organization and researchers who are outsiders, with the aim of both addressing relevant organizational issues and creating practical knowledge about organizational change through the partnership and through the dialogical process by creating generative images and shared understanding. It takes place in the present tense and the role of the researcher is that of an engaged scholar enacting humble inquiry. We have provided a concrete example in the vignette. In the next chapter we explore the theoretical foundations of collaborative inquiry in organization development and change.

2. Theoretical foundations

In Chapter 1 we introduced the elements of collaborative inquiry in terms of conversations between those who are insiders to the organization and those who are outsiders, with the aim of both addressing relevant organizational issues and creating practical knowledge about organizational change though a partnership and a dialogical process by creating generative images and shared understanding. It takes place in the present tense and the role of the researcher is that of an engaged scholar enacting humble inquiry. In this chapter we fill out the background and introduce the core constructs of organization learning and organization development within a social science philosophy; collaborative inquiry; the essence of partnership; Mode 1 and Mode 2 knowledge production and meaning creation in their historical organization development (OD) context and how they have developed; and a philosophy of practical knowing and inquiring in the present tense. Figure 2.1 captures the main theoretical foundations and key concepts.

ORGANIZATIONS AS LEARNING SYSTEMS

Chapter 1 identified organizational learning as one of the core elements of collaborative inquiry. As learning is an integral part of any living system (de Geus, 1998; March, 1991) one can tease out a wide variety of organizational learning facets. For example, learning can be explored as an individual, group, organizational, inter-organizational or network phenomenon (Lipshitz et al., 2007; Coughlan & Coghlan, 2011); there are different levels of learning such as single loop, double loop and deutero learning cycles and adaptive generative (Senge, 1990; Argyris & Schon, 1996); learning as technical and social processes (Gavin, 2000; Shani & Docherty, 2003); and learning as content vs. process vs. contextual phenomenon (Cohen & Sproull, 1996; Kolb, 1984).

The origin of the organization learning conceptualization is anchored in the synthesis of contemporary theories that include system theory, adaptive complex system, sociotechnical systems, group behavior, human development and individual learning theories. The literature on

Figure 2.1   The theoretical foundations of collaborative inquiry

individual learning within organizations is considerable and runs through most of the streams of educational, psychological and organizational behavior research (Friedman et al., 2001). The literature on organizational learning runs through the organizational science, sociological, economics, and organization change and development research (Antal et al., 2001).

While a myriad of views of what organization learning is about appear in the literature, Argyris and Schon (1996:16) for example, state that "organization learning occurs when individuals within an organization experience a problematic situation and inquire into it on behalf of the organization." According to Senge (1990: 16) ". . . organizations where people continually expand their capacity to create the results they truly desire, where new and expansive patterns of thinking are nurtured, where collectives' aspirations are set free, and where people are continually learning how to learn together." For Dixon (1999: 6), it is ". . . the intentional use of learning processes at the individual, group and system level to continuously transform the organization in a direction that is increasingly satisfying to its stakeholders." The central elements contained in these accounts of organizational learning, particularly expressed by Senge, are, in our view, at the heart of collaborative inquiry.

As social entities within a dynamic business context, organizations need to continue to refine and develop learning capabilities. As we have shown, many different theories and perspectives about organization learning can be found in the literature. Attempts to cluster and group the theories and perspectives have been made, yet such a review is beyond the scope of this book. For our purpose we adopt Shani and Docherty's (2003) three complementary groups of learning mechanisms, according to the evolutions of a stream of research that is placed on a historical timeline (the late 1940s and early 1950s; the late 1950s; the late 1960s; the early 1990s); first- and second-order learning based on impact (1st and 2nd order of learning); and based on level of learning typologies (Type I – the correction of deviations, Type II – the examination of assumptions, and Type III –learning-to-learn problem solving).

Learning Mechanisms

Learning mechanisms are viewed as a formal configuration – structures, processes, procedures, rules, tools, methods, and physical or virtual space – created within or outside an organization for the purpose of developing, enhancing and sustaining innovation, performance and learning (Bushe & Shani, 1991; Popper & Lipshitz, 1998; Cirella et al., 2016). A combination of learning mechanisms may be viewed as a tapestry that develops organically through the maturation of an organization as a complex adaptive system. Just as there are many types of structures, processes and procedures, they are also various ways to map out, enhance, design and re-design learning mechanisms (Shani & Docherty, 2008).

A critical element of learning is the need for a space in which learning occurs. The need for "space" for learning – or knowledge creation – was advanced by Nonaka and Konno (1998), based on the concept of *ba* that was originally developed by the Japanese philosopher Kitaro Nishida. *Ba* is defined as a context in which knowledge is shared, created and utilized, in recognition that knowledge needs a context in order to exist. Nonaka et al. (2001) claim that *ba* does not necessarily mean a physical space. They suggest that it can be a physical space (i.e., an office space), a virtual space (i.e., a teleconference), a mental space (shared ideas), or any combination of these kind of spaces. A critical aspect of *ba* is space for interaction. As such, *ba* is viewed as interaction between individuals, between individuals and the environment, and between individuals and information, but not necessarily the space itself. Friedman et al. (2016) emphasize the need to create social space that enables individuals ". . . to think, feel, and act in ways that exercise greater choice over the realities they construct and construct them." Learning mechanisms provide the space and the context where collaborative inquiry takes place, and learning and change are created. Lastly, Schein and Schein (2019) emphasize the centrality of a sense of psychological safety in the social space for learning and change to occur.

ORGANIZATION DEVELOPMENT AND CHANGE

The term organization development and change (commonly referred to as ODC) refers to an approach to organizational change that is a philosophy, a professional field of social action, a mode of scientific inquiry and an array of approaches to enable change and learning to take place in organizations (Beer, 1980; Cummings, 2008; Schein, 2010; Burnes & Cooke, 2012). It is understood to be somewhat different from what is often referred to as change management which emerged from organization development and became associated with expert-based prescription, especially by large consulting firms. It is understood to refer to a specific values-based approach that has its roots in the work of Kurt Lewin, Eric Trist and Fred Emery, and is deeply embedded in participative management, sensitivity training, action research and sociotechnical systems.

One of the earliest definitions was provided by Beckhard (1969: 9) a founder of OD, as "an effort (1) planned, (2) organization-wide, (3) managed from the top, to (4) increase organization effectiveness and health through (5) planned interventions in the organization's processes using behavioral-science knowledge." In their best-selling textbook, French and Bell (1990: 17) provide a more elaborate definition which states that "organization development is a long-range effort to improve an organization's problem-solving and renewal processes, particularly through a more effective and collaborative management of organization culture – with special emphasis on the culture of formal work teams

– with the assistance of a change agent or catalyst and the use of the theory and technology of applied behavioral science, including action research." More recently, Beer (2014: 60) provided a collaborative-based and systemwide-based view which states that "organization development is a system-wide process of data collection, diagnosis, action planning, intervention, and evaluation aimed at: (1) enhancing congruence between organizational structure, process, strategy, people, and culture; (2) developing new and creative organizational solutions; and (3) developing the organization's self-renewing capacity. It occurs through collaboration of organizational members working with a change agent using behavioral science theory, research, and technology."

There have been multiple definitions of ODC across the decades, as can be seen above, but they tend to comprise the following elements in one form or other: that it is a long-term effort whose aim is to improve an organization's processes of renewing itself through discovering and envisioning its future, structuring itself appropriately, being able to solve problems and transferring transformation skills to the organization. The ODC process is embedded in a collaborative inquiry process that is enriched by commitment to dialogical and conversational practices. ODC places special emphasis on an ongoing management of organizational culture, particularly in work teams and interdepartmental configurations. It may utilize an external OD consultant who works in a facilitator role, rather than an expert advisor role (Schein, 1969) or it may be practiced by an organizational insider (Coghlan, 2019).

The field of organization development and change emerged from the increasing demands of the evolving social and business environment coupled with the emerging applied behavioral science knowledge (Friedlander & Brown, 1974; Burnes & Cooke, 2012). While the practice of organization development was emerging in the 1960s and was named as such by practitioners such as Robert Blake and Richard Beckhard, respectively, its establishment as a distinctive field is considered to be marked by the publication of the Addison-Wesley OD series in 1969. The initial six books of the series laid out the wide range of approaches that comprise the field of OD. The series later expanded to comprise over thirty volumes, capturing the broad plurality of approaches within the emerging field. As co-founder and co-editor of the series, Schein (2009a) later reflected that, if they were to launch a further series, they would find the need for several books rather than for a single text.

The field of organization development and change holds a rather unique place in social science and in organization studies because of its dual and eclectic nature (Coghlan et al., 2019). This dual identity joins a science of organizational change and an art of changing organizations (Woodman, 2014). At its core, the field evolved around collaborative human inquiry, for the purpose of continuously improving living systems. From its emergence in the 1950s, ODC and human inquiry have always been driven by academic rigor and practical relevance as it is practiced by both a scholar and a consultant community. Schein (2010: 93) described the emergence of OD as a "quiet revolution," on which he elaborated: "what created OD was a combination of a new inquiry approach based on a willingness to gather data in the field by non-traditional methods, with the vivid concerns of a set of practitioners who wanted to improve organizations."

Action research is one of the distinctive features of organization development and one of its core origins (Coghlan, 2012; Burnes & Cooke, 2012). In its traditional form, action research used in organization development is based on collaboration between a behavioral scientist-researcher and the client, where they collaborate on intervening in the organization (the action), and in exploring issues and generating data on the development of the organization (the research activity). The insight underpinning action research may be found in the insights attributed to Lewin that there can be no research without action and no action without research, and that it was not enough to try to explain things; one also had to try to change them. As Schein (2010) notes, these insights led to the development of action research and the powerful notion that organizations could be understood and changed only if one involved the members of the system in the inquiry process itself. In Schein's view, action research was based on two assumptions which are the cornerstones of organization development: that involving the clients or learners in their own learning not only produces better learning but more valid data about how the system really works, and that one only understands a system when one tries to change it, as changing organizations often involves variables which cannot be controlled by traditional research methods.

The evolution of the OD field over the past 70 years has witnessed the development of a wide variety of approaches, methods and philosophies that have centered on the development of systems, whatever and wherever they were situated. Over the years, as methods, approaches and orientations have emerged, so did attempts to cluster, group and categorize them (Coghlan et al., 2019). The debate about social science and social science philosophical orientations has led to a few clusters of approaches, such as Mode 1 and Mode 2 knowledge production practices that further sharpen the nature and distinct character of the emerging field.

One of the contextual forces for the emergence of organization development was the growing sense of the inadequacy of the bureaucratic model of organization. Bennis (1969), in one of the first books on organization development, presents the construct of mechanistic and organistic organizational systems, originally described by Burns and Stalker (1961). Mechanistic systems are those in which the emphasis is on authority–obedience relationships, strict division of labor, centralized decision-making and conflict resolution through suppression, arbitration and/or warfare. Organistic systems are based on the image of the organization as a living organism, where there is emphasis on interdependence and shared responsibility, mutual confidence and trust, wide sharing of responsibility and control, multi-group membership and responsibility, and conflict resolution through bargaining or problem-solving. In Bennis' view, the mechanistic system is threatened by rapid and unexpected change, as the organization's ability to respond to a changing world is lessened by its inflexibility and rigidity.

Organization development has always espoused inquiry *with* people rather than *on* or *for* them in the process of creating new meaning and actions. The *with* people collaborative inquiry foundational orientation of ODC is embedded in relationship building, a willingness to challenge prevailing assumptions, dialogue and reflexivity. The social science knowledge domain implies that inquiry with people is a collaborative discovery process in the creation of new meaning. At the heart of most ODC work there is commitment to the generation of new meaning that is based in honest conversations, dialogue and reflexivity that guides practice. Dialogue is a process in which all participants are open to the possibility of being changed by the other, perhaps in uncomfortable ways, while reflexivity is the process of critical self-questioning which facilitates the dialogue to be authentic.

Organization development and change, in its essence, is founded on both dialogical and collaboration foundations. In most ODC efforts, the dialogical aspect refers to dialogue between managers and researchers, and through the collaborative inquiry process, meaning is created from the data reviews that then impact managerial decisions. According to research by Shani et al. (2012: 53), "Collaboration implies research efforts that include the active involvement of members of a living system and researchers in the framing and re-framing of the improvement agenda, the exploration, selection and pursuit of methods and the development of implications for action." In order for the collaborative effort to work, each party must engage in collective inquiry through dialogue and share a fundamental interest in learning.

CONVERSATION AND DIALOGUE IN ORGANIZATION DEVELOPMENT AND CHANGE

Dialogue and conversations have been a central process and an integral foundational element in the field of organization development and change since its origin. At the most basic level the concept and practice of dialogue is not complicated. Dialogue is a good conversation between two or more individuals. Dialogue is also a form of free exchange of ideas, information and meaning between individuals (Bohm, 1989). As time progresses, humans tend to exchange thoughtful ideas about things that matter more. According to Brown (1995: 156), ". . . it is about creating the space to be together and talk, as the ideas and thoughts come to us, without agenda, without time pressure." Dialogue, as a concept, is rooted in both Greek philosophy and contemporary thought leaders. In the Greek tradition, for example, the Socratic dialogue was a way for the master to push students for a greater level of wisdom. In contemporary organization and management literature, Senge (1990) for example, argues that the dialogical process is a central process for system thinking and system learning. According to Palus and Drath (2001: 7), "dialogue at its best is a way of creating profound levels of shared meaning in a group so that the wisest course of action can emerge." Beer (2020) advanced the concept of "honest dialogue" or "honest conversations" as critical for successful organization development and change initiatives.

Bushe and Marshak (2009, 2014, 2015) introduced the concept of "dialogic organization development" and differentiated it from "diagnostic organization development" which they claimed was dominant in the earlier work, ideas and practices in the field. They further argue that the two represent two different mindsets: one is embedded in "the right problem identification," "the right answer," "best solution," "best way of organizing," "latest idea," and "planned change process," while the other is embedded in "social construction of reality," "generative image creation," "narrative creation," "emergent change process," and "self-organizing complex adaptive systems." Yet, since its inception, the field of organization development was committed to addressing an organizational issue and simultaneously creating new knowledge. As such, polarization of the "dialogic" and "diagnostic" was rarely the focus of the work, but rather the drive to generate valid data upon which actions could be taken and simultaneously studied. While collaborative inquiry is philosophically grounded in the dialogic organization development mindset with its emphasis on the collaborative conversations between the partners, some elements of diagnostic OD are pertinent as judgments are made about the effectiveness of strategies, structures and processes. As Coghlan et al. (2020) point out, Mode 1 methods may be used within a Mode 2 philosophy, so diagnostic methods may be used within a dialogic OD mindset.

As we introduced in Chapter 1, the distinct dynamic of development and change efforts – grounded in a philosophy of practical knowing – place an emphasis on inquiring in the present tense (Coghlan & Shani, 2017). The dialogical and conversational process between members of the system imply that individuals suspend assumptions about what is "right" and inquire together into their own ways of thinking, to collectively discover new insights and to reflect on their own assumptions that led to their own belief systems (Friedman et al., 2016). The dialogic perspective can be examined through Gergen's (1978: 1344) lens of generative theory, which frames theory as a "capacity to challenge prevailing assumptions regarding the nature of social life and to offer fresh alternatives to contemporary patterns of conduct." Collaborative inquiry aims to do just that, to change an organization's prevailing assumptions and actions, transform mindsets, create a new collective mindset, learn new strategies, and actions and organizing alternatives to what the organization does.

PARTNERSHIPS

As can be seen in Chapter 1, partnerships seem to be at the core of collaborative inquiry in dialogic organization development. By their very nature, partnerships between humans are complex to design, manage or facilitate. Yet, partnership life-cycles in organizational life are common (Galuppo et al., 2019). Organization structures and processes by their very nature create the context for partnerships at work. For our purpose, partners are those individuals, groups or organizations who have an interest in the action of an organization and who desire to influence it (Freeman et al., 2010; Shani et al., 2008). Partnerships tend to develop over time, go through stages of development and evolve as distinct types (Gray, 1989; Mirvis & Googins, 2006). Selsky and Parker (2010), for example, identified three kinds of partnerships: transactional, developmental and integrative. *Transactional partnerships* tend to be short-term, limited in focus and resources, where each partner is pressured to solve their own mission-related problems and performance needs. *Developmental partnerships* tend to be long-term oriented, open-ended in terms of focus and resources, where each partner is invested in a long-term added-value relationship, less concerned in solving a specific problem and seeing the opportunity to develop a new vision and creation of a new organization. As such, the developmental partnership tends to be more idealistic oriented. Like developmental partnership, *integrative partnerships* tend to be long-term oriented, yet focused on specific issues. In this orientation type, each partner is interested in keeping the organization performance goals in balance with the achievement of common and shared issues. The different kinds, levels and mindset orientation of partnerships' logic are likely to have a different view and impact of the collaborative inquiry process and outcomes.

COLLABORATIVE INQUIRY

The broad conceptual framework presented in Chapter 1 places collaborative inquiry as central to most ODC work (see Figure 1.1). The framework in Figure 1.1 is based on the assumption and understanding of organizations as social constructions held together by shared meanings. It involves a partnership between researchers and practitioners who work together in a mode of engaged scholarship and humble inquiry. It is focused on addressing real issues and generating practical knowledge. Next, we explore further the essence of collaboration.

Collaboration

Collaboration encompasses a full range of partnerships and relationships among individuals, groups and organizations (Hay & Samra-Fredericks, 2019; Mattessich & Johnson, 2018). In the context of ODC, collaboration implies change and research efforts which include the active engagement of members of the living system and researchers in the framing of the action and research agenda, the selection and pursuit of methods, and the development of actionable implications. Collaboration requires collective inquiry, the joint pursuit of answers to questions of mutual interest through dialogue, experimentation, the review and integration of knowledge, or other means (Shani et al., 2017). Members of a system engage in collective inquiry in order to better understand a certain issue or phenomenon using scientifically valid knowledge and methods. Similarly, researchers engage in collective inquiry in order to better understand a certain issue or phenomena using practically valid knowledge from practitioners. Collaboration does not impose the requirement of an equal partnership in each of these activities, although we posit that a more equal partnership better supports the fulfillment of dialogic OD's multiple objectives (Bartunek & Rynes, 2014; Friedman et al., 2016).

Collaborative relationships are at the center of collaborative inquiry. The nature and quality of *collaborative relationships* have the most significant impact on the phases of knowledge production and its outcomes (Gray, 1989; Hibbert & Huxham, 2005). Collaboration between scholars and practitioners through the OD project enhances management decision-making, generating new and relevant knowledge about emerging issues and possible future business directions by integrating insights from organizational members in a scientific way. The quality of collaboration depends upon the collaborative mechanisms – what we framed earlier as learning mechanisms – that are designed and managed. Thompson et al. (2009) suggest that higher levels of reciprocal autonomy and mutuality yield opportunities for more intense collaboration.

Mohrman and Shani (2008) theorized that collaborative relationships depend on four factors: the institutional and resource contexts of collaboration, alignment of purpose between the different actors (namely academics and practitioners), the mechanisms that enable learning in collaborative relationships, and the convergence of the languages of practice and theory. While the institutional and resource contexts in which collaboration takes places are partially exogenous and thus less under the control of project partners, collaborators actively strive to create a common definition of critical issues and to agree on the scope of research.

During early dialogue, collaborators typically explore different ways to undertake a project including the composition of appropriate learning mechanisms and/or the enhancement of learning mechanisms that are already a part of the organization. For example, the possible creation of a project steering group and/or study teams to guide the project, the organization and study focus. The steering group develops processes to guide itself and the study team(s), determines how collaborators interact with organizational members that are not directly involved in the research, identifies appropriate coordination mechanisms, and develops mechanisms to address unanticipated challenges. Collaborators must consider the make-up of the study team(s) including diversity (e.g., demographics, motivation, personality), the number of organizational and academic members, the structure and roles of the team(s) and individual members, necessary resources, and the further development of a shared vision. The climate is also an integral part of collaborative relationships (Cross et al., 2018). Nurturing a collaborative climate requires modeling concern, a learning orientation, trust, openness and mutual respect. Furthermore, the collaborators must foster the development and maintenance of skills and competencies needed to fulfill the goals of the project. The complex nature of any business context coupled with intent to transform the organization suggests the need for sensitive structural configurations and processes that sustain the academic–practitioner partnerships (Shani & Docherty, 2003). According to a design perspective, the partners create a tapestry of cognitive, structural and procedural learning mechanisms (Docherty & Shani, 2008) to fit a particular collaboration. The exploration of learning mechanisms and the design of possible supplemental learning mechanisms will be explored in Chapter 4.

Generativity

Generativity "is an adjective meaning the power to generate, produce, originate" (Bushe & Marshak, 2020: 22). A distinctive feature of early OD work that was further advanced by sociotechnical system thinking and dialogic OD was that transformational system change requires new ways of thinking, creative ideas, different forums and ways of dialogue, and commitment to change, development and improvement. Bushe's (2013) research found that generative images capabilities are central to appreciative inquiry. Press, Bellis et al.'s (2020) research, which is embedded in design science research orientation (i.e., Dresch et al., 2014; Collatto et al., 2017) and focused on work, design-driven innovation and leadership, found that the design of objects is critical in triggering a dialogue that is critical for transformation in the digital era. Coupling both perspectives puts generativity at the center of collaborative inquiry.

Foundational to generativity is the notion that humans are driven by the creation of objects and meaning for themselves, for relevant others, for their systems and society. Meaning can be viewed as the internal cognitive and emotional structures of ideas and feelings that allow a person to understand a version of the world, manifest as a representation of the way things are and the way they ought be, and that places the person into this world version. Bartunek (1984) advanced the concept of "interpretive schemas" and argues that cognitive schemes are used to map up human's experience, identify what is relevant and how to understand the experience. In this context, we see that meaning can be seen as the naming, interpreting, and making commitments to act with other people. Press, Bellis et al.'s (2020) study suggests that people are quite engaged when they make things – words, stories, pictures, artifacts. As such, space needs to be created where individuals feel safe to engage in making things collectively and interpreting their meaning (Schein & Schein, 2019).

Simon, in his influential book, *The Sciences of the Artificial* (1996: 113) claims that a science of design is ". . . a body of intellectual tough, analytic, partly formalize, partly empirical, teachable doctrine about the design process." He further argues that "everyone designs" and as such design thinking and practice being a natural human process should become an integral part of discovery and work. The design science research school of thought tends to emphasize the creation of objects or artifacts as the trigger for meaning-making. This perspective is based on the assumption that conversations that are triggered by the designed object or artifact creates the space for the sharing of individuals' cognitive schemas and the beginning of the creation of a new and shared collective schema. These representations reflect an individual's and collective knowledge, perception, and understanding of what is and what should be, and therefore are meaningful.

Collaborative inquiry is first and foremost a process of negotiating meaning (Wenger, 1998). Meaning can be viewed as the internal cognitive and emotional structures containing coded information that allows a person to understand their version of the world (Solari et al., 2015). Innovation of meaning was first introduced by Verganti (2009) as a strategy aimed at radically changing the reason why people use a product or a service, acting not only on the utilitarian, but also on the symbolic and emotional dimensions. In other words, this approach aims to change the meaning of products and services through a deep understanding of broader changes in society, culture and technology. Rather than being pulled by user requirements, transformation is pushed by a firm's vision about possible new product meanings and languages that could diffuse in society. Verganti (2017: 14) argues that since ". . . Everyone in her heart nurtures a sense of direction, a hypothesis of what people would love . . . by exposing this inkling of hypothesis, we make our cognitive frame explicit; we make it visible to others who can then target it and challenge it (through) . . . criticism nurtured by a common will to move beyond old interpretations . . . to a new shared vision."

At the core of creating meaning is sense-making (Solari et al., 2015; Ravasi and Stigliani, 2012; Weick, 1995). We arrange our understanding of experience so that we can know what has happened and what is happening, and so that we can predict what will happen; it is constructing knowledge of ourselves and the world. Meaning and community are engaging because they are co-constructive. When making such structures happen in a community/practice (people united in a common enterprise who share history and thus certain values, beliefs, ways of talking and ways of doing things), transformation is feasible. Therefore, meaning-making is all about constructing a sense of what is, and what is important for collective action (Drath & Palus, 1994). If development is seen as collective sense-making, creating the space for creation, discovery and interpretation is likely to result in new human experience that leads to the creation of new meaning that will be acted upon.

MODE 2 KNOWLEDGE CREATION AND COLLABORATIVE INQUIRY

As we suggested earlier in Chapter 1, the foundation of collaborative inquiry is its orientation to creating knowledge. Following Gibbons et al.'s (1994) classification of scientific approaches and methods into two clusters of knowledge production, namely Mode 1 and Mode 2 orientations, and not staying within the debate of knowledge production that continues to dominate social and organization sciences, we argue that collaborative inquiry fits more within Mode 2 than Mode 1 orientations (Coghlan et al., 2020).

Gibbons et al. (1994) describe what might be understood as research in traditional terms, producing explanatory knowledge universal knowledge through building and testing theory within a disciplinary field by drawing causal inferences from the data to test hypotheses which are validated by logic, measurement, and consistency of prediction and control. The role of the researcher is that of an observer and the relationship to the setting is detached and neutral. In contrast, Gibbons and colleagues present Mode 2 as the "new" knowledge production. They describe five main characteristics that distinguish it from Mode 1. Mode 2 knowledge is generated in the *context of* application. It is *transdisciplinary*, and mobilizes a range of theoretical perspectives and practical methodologies to address issues. Mode 2 knowledge production is *reflexive*, through a dialogic process and by being sensitive to the research process itself, and incorporates multiple views. *Quality controls* are grounded in how the research approach is collaborative and produces consequential outcomes. Mode 2 knowledge producers are concerned with addressing concrete issues and produce generalizable knowledge only as a by-product.

From this brief introduction to Mode 2 knowledge production it can be seen how the definition and elements of collaborative inquiry, which we described in Chapter 1, are in accord with Mode 2. Both Mode 2 and collaborative inquiry research combines theoretical knowledge with applied, practical knowledge to address particular organizational issues and to generate practical knowledge. In contrast to Mode 1 knowledge researchers, who seek to find generalizable laws across contexts by taking a disengaged, scientific approach, collaborative inquiry Mode 2 researchers are closely tied to applied contexts and are charged with achieving concrete results by creating actionable knowledge that can advance organizational causes and produce practical knowledge. Their point of contact is closer to practice and involves investigating problems of high interest and practical import that sometimes cut across disciplines (Van de Ven, 2007; Shani et al., 2008; Mohrman et al., 2011; Coghlan et al., 2020). Table 2.1 captures the key features of Mode 1 and Mode 2 research orientations.

COLLABORATIVE INQUIRY IN THE PRESENT TENSE

The ground on which a collaborative inquiry initiative is founded is the context of a social space where through shared inquiry and deliberate action a change takes place. Within that social space an array of complex engagements takes place. These occur between researchers and organizational members over time, between the researchers themselves and between organizational members, as they experience events, work to understand them, verify their understanding and make judgments on the basis of which they make decisions and take action. Parallel to these collaborative activities are the individual cognitional and valuing operations in which individuals engage as they experience events, work to understand them, verify their understanding and make judgments on the basis of which they make decisions and take action in their teams. There are also the tasks of meeting the goal to co-generate and disseminate actionable knowledge, that is, knowledge that is useful for practice and robust for scholars beyond the specifics of the particular organization in which the inquiry is taking place. Attentiveness in the present keeps an eye to the quality of how these engagements are enacted. While in

Table 2.1   Modes 1 and 2 knowledge production

	Mode 1	Mode 2
Aim of research	Universal knowledge in quantitative studies Theory building and testing within a discipline for qualitative studies	Co-generated practical knowledge produced in the transdisciplinary context of the application
Type of knowledge produced	Universal knowledge in quantitative studies	Practical knowledge from particular situation that's transportable to like settings
Nature of data	Context free Context located	Emergent in the context of intervention
Validation	Logic, measurement, consistency of prediction and control External & internal validity	Experiential Collaborative transdisciplinary through the collaborative transformation process
Researcher's role	Observer/data analyst	Engaged scholar in transdisciplinary partnership Accountable to the organization as well as to academic field
Researcher's relationship to setting	Detached, neutral	Immersed, engaged Reflexive
Ways of Knowing	Propositional	Practical

Chapter 3 we describe the operations of how we come to know as comprising experience, understanding and judgment, with judgment of value and decision when action follows, here we advert to how our knowing unfolds in the present tense.

WAYS OF KNOWING

While the process of our human knowing is invariant, that is, through the operations of experience, understanding and judgment, as we will describe in Chapter 3, we enact these operations differently in different settings, for instance in a laboratory or in an art gallery. We are familiar with these; how, for example, when we listen to music, read poetry or visit an art gallery, we are in a presentational or aesthetic form of knowing as we appreciate melodies and harmonies, language or visual representations. We engage in a different way of knowing when we are engaged in science and are studying technical documents or assessing financial reports. Here we adopt a scientific form of knowing as we check data and weigh evidence and conclusions. Relational knowing is what we draw on when we work with someone or form a friendship. Then there is the realm of practical knowing that enables us to manage our everyday activities, to which we apply our intelligence to practical tasks. In each of these settings the insights we receive are in a different form and we process them differently. Heron and Reason (1997) argue that practical knowing is primary as it integrates other forms of knowing. We draw on the knowledge created by others and use it intelligently, for example when we cook a meal. The recipe in the cookbook provides the theory but then we have to apply it intelligently in order that the meal is tasty. In our organizational world, for example, we can draw on operations management theory to effect changes in how the operation of the supply chain might be improved, but what to do and how to do it takes us into the realm of practical knowing. As we will explore in Chapters 3 and 4, creating generative imagery is an important activity in collaborative inquiry and requires attention be paid to the process of coming to know.

In his reflection on the emergence of modernity from the Renaissance period, Toulmin (1990) comments that modernism split the knower from the known and avoided the issue of the subject in his/her acts of consciousness. Consequently, the subject became neglected and excluded from management and organizational research. He notes that from 1630 on, the focus of philosophical inquiries ignored the particular, concrete, timely and local details of everyday human affairs and instead shifted to a higher, stratospheric plane, on which nature and ethics conformed to abstract, timeless, general and universal theories. He concludes that "today this theoretical agenda is wearing out its welcome and the philosophical problems of practice are coming back into focus" (p. 186). Toulmin's critique echoes the elaboration of the difference between diagnostic and dialogic OD framed by Bushe and Marshak (2015).

THE PHILOSOPHY OF PRACTICAL KNOWING

In the context of the neglect and denigration of practical knowing in the academy, Coghlan (2016) frames a philosophy of practical knowing in terms of four characteristics: (a) our knowing in this mode is concerned with the everyday concerns of human living, (b) much of our knowing in this mode is socially derived, constructed and reconstructed continuously, (c) we need to attend to the uniqueness of each situation and (d) our practical knowing and action is driven by values and is fundamentally ethical in that as we take practical action we are constantly making judgments about what is the appropriate or best thing to do. We now elaborate on these four characteristics.

The Everyday Concerns of Human Living

Collaborative inquiry does not pursue knowledge for its own sake but it pursues actions that are judged to be worthwhile. In the context of business and management, everyday practical concerns are about issues such as survival, productivity, effectiveness, customer service, improvement and change. Those who undertake collaborative inquiry do so not merely to study such issues but to improve or transform the organization and its operations.

Knowing is Socially Constructed

As referred to above, we understand how the creation of institutions and their operations are socially constructed; that is, they are creations of the human mind and are designed and run to achieve intended purposes. Consequently, when participants engage in collaborative inquiry they experience that others interpret situations differently and accordingly engage in dialogical and collaborative activities which seek to build common understanding and consensual collaborative action.

Attending to the Uniqueness of Each Situation

The third characteristic of practical knowing is that it requires attentiveness to the uniqueness of each situation, that is, it takes place in the present tense. We have discussed this earlier in this chapter. What this particular characteristic of practical knowing means is that knowing varies from place to place and from situation to situation. What worked in one setting or worked at an earlier time may not work now. No two situations are identical. Remembering what worked before is an insight into situations which are similar but not identical. What took place on a previous occasion is irretrievable and obsolete and has to be revisited and modified in the light of the present unique situation. If the uniqueness of the present situation is ignored then there is a serious threat to learning and changing. Common statements such as "We have done this before so we know how to do it now" or "we have always done it this way" need to be challenged. Therefore, our practical knowing needs be differentiated for each specific situation and, as collaborative researchers, we need to be attentive in the present tense and engage in listening, questioning and testing assumptions as the project unfolds.

Practical Knowing and Action is Value-driven and Ethical

Practical action is driven by values, that is, what we judge to be worth doing, and so is fundamentally ethical in how values and goals are identified, choices are made and actions are taken. As collaborative inquiry is conducted in the present tense, attentiveness to these choices and their consequences, and being transparent about them, are significant in considering the quality of collaborative inquiry. We will discuss quality in Chapter 5.

CONCLUSIONS

In Chapter 1 we introduced the fundamental elements of collaborative inquiry in terms of conversations between those who are insiders to the organization and those who are outsiders with the aim of both addressing relevant organizational issues and creating practical knowledge about organizational change though the partnership and through the dialogical process by creating generative images and shared understanding. This chapter has focused on the theoretical foundations of collaborative inquiry in organization development. In Chapter 1 we presented the overall framework. In this chapter we have provided the theoretical background and captured the key elements in the framework (see Figure 2.1). The collaborative inquiry in an organization development framework builds on the view of organizations as social systems, organizations as learning systems, organization development and change within a social science philosophy, the essence of partnership, inquiry in the present tense, and an inquiry orientation that fits more within the domain of Mode 2 knowledge production process practice. We have advocated that such inquiry, dialogue and conversations take place in the present tense and the role of the scholar-practitioner is that of an engaged scholar enacting humble inquiry.

3. Methodology and methods of inquiry

In Chapter 1 we introduced the fundamentals of collaborative inquiry as conversations or dialogues between organizational members and external researchers aimed at addressing relevant organizational issues and creating practical knowledge about organizational change. We outlined the history of organization development and change and showed how, from its inception, it has engaged with the twin tasks of articulating a social science of change and processes of changing (Woodman, 2014). In Chapter 2, we provided the theoretical foundations and key concepts of collaborative inquiry. Building on Mode 2 orientation, in this chapter we introduce and describe a general empirical method for engaging in collaborative inquiry, a method that is built on the recognizable activities of human knowing. As such, the method of collaborative inquiry should be viewed as an applied research (vs basic or fundamental research), that is, within the Mode 2 knowledge creation domain, but also an orientation that utilizes some Mode 1 methods, as needed during the inquiry process (Coghlan et al., 2020). Figure 3.1 captures the key elements in this chapter.

This method – be attentive to experience; be intelligent in envisaging possible explanations of the experience; be reasonable in preferring as probable or certain the explanations that provide the best account for the experience; and be responsible for one's actions – underpins the collaborative inquiry orientation of organization development (OD) as it seeks to generate the practical knowledge of improving and changing organizations. Later in the chapter we explore how collaborative inquiry has become a general term and is used to refer to a family of approaches or modalities and how each modality offers insight into the process of inquiry. The last section is devoted to discussion of some of the ethical challenges in the methodological orientation of collaborative inquiry.

Organization development and change engages members in interpreting events and the variety of actions that envisage ends, in selecting means, evaluating outcomes and capturing learning. It works by criti-

Figure 3.1   Methodology and methods of collaborative inquiry

quing these ends, by understanding how these ends are achieved, and by deciding whether members want to achieve these or other ends. The conversations focus on strategies and actions, how participants figure out what they mean, how they are understood, what is considered to be of value and what might need to be done, and what happens when change is attempted and what might be learned. The collaborative inquiry process engages participants in discussing the multiple meanings that exist in a collective venture and seeks to enable participants to express the meanings they hold, listen to and understand, and to appreciate the meanings other participants hold and to create new meaning in response to external and internal opportunities and threats.

THE DYNAMIC STRUCTURE OF HUMAN KNOWING

In light of our understanding that organizations are constructed and maintained through acts of common meaning, our starting point is the structure of human knowing because it is how we come to know and to value that is at the basis of how we construct and understand the world in which we live and seek to shape.

The structure of human knowing may be understood as a dynamic three-step process: experience, understanding and judgment (Lonergan, 1992; Cronin, 2017). Experience takes place at the empirical level of consciousness and is an interaction of outer and inner events, or data of sense and data of consciousness. We not only experience external data through our five senses, i.e., what we hear, see, smell, taste and touch, but we also experience internal data as we think, feel, remember and imagine. We also experience ourselves as seeing, hearing, thinking, feeling, remembering and imagining. For instance, we can be aware how we are excited while watching a film or be aware of ourselves being moved as we listen to music or poetry. Sensory data are what we experience but do not yet understand. What is that noise? Is it raining? So we ask questions, and the answers come in the form of insights, which are acts of understanding, of grasping and formulating patterns, unities, relationships and explanations in response to the questions posed to our experience. The noise sounds like the phone ringing. The water running down the window means it is raining. While we might not know yet if a particular current search is intelligent, we anticipate intelligent answers. Insight or understanding occurs at the intellectual level of consciousness as we move beyond description to explanation. The noise we hear is the phone ringing. Yet, while insights are common they are not always accurate, correct or satisfactory answers to our questions. The question then is, is the insight correct or does it provide a satisfactory answer to the question posed to experience? This opens up a question for reflection. Is it so? Yes or no? Maybe. We don't know. We can check and affirm that the noise is that of the phone ringing. We can affirm that it is raining and the water on the window is not due to a leak overhead. Accordingly, we move to a new level of the cognitional process, where we marshal and weigh evidence and assess its sufficiency and judge that it is definitely/probably true or not. We are at the rational level of consciousness. This pattern is invariant in that it applies to all settings of cognitional activity, whether solving an everyday problem or engaging in scientific research. To reject or dismiss this pattern involves experience, understanding and judging and, paradoxically, confirms it.

At the same time we know it doesn't work like this all the time. We know that there are such things as obtuseness, narrowmindedness, confusion, lack of attention and bias. We may not bother to ask questions about our experience. An understanding may not come quickly enough, and we may be impatient and not question further. Many insights may be wrong. Interpretations of data may be superficial, inaccurate or biased. Judgments may be flawed. We may have unconscious fears which censor, block or divert questioning. We can be egotistical where we use our intelligence to figure out how to exploit people. We can be blind to the limitations of our culture, race, gender and of the groups with which we identify. Accordingly, we need to gain insight into these negative manifestations of knowing by using the same threefold process of knowing.

We do not merely know facts, i.e., that it is raining or that the phone is ringing. We also make decisions and act (the responsible level of consciousness). The process here is that we add the activities of valuing, choosing, deciding, and taking action to the cognitive operations of experiencing, understanding, and judging what is known. At this level we ask what courses of action are open to us and we review options, weigh choices and decide. We may reflect on the possible value judgments as to what the best option might be and we decide to follow through in action. A judgment that the noise we heard was the phone ringing is a judgment of fact. A judgment that an action is good/bad, right/wrong, appropriate/ inappropriate, worthwhile or not is a judgment of value. We return to the process of valuing and ethics later in this chapter.

Of course, the factual outcomes of questioning whether it is raining or not or whether the noise was or was not the phone ringing are not replicated when we try to know the world of human behavior and social structures. As we discussed earlier, this world is mediated by meaning which constitutes human living. We learn to construct our respective worlds by giving meaning to data that continuously impinge on us from within ourselves and as well as from without. Meaning goes beyond experiencing, as what is meant is not only experienced but is also something we seek to understand and to affirm. There is the task of seeking to understand the many meanings that constitute organizations and social structures, expressed in language, in symbols and in actions. Accordingly, we inquire into how values, behavior and assumptions are socially constructed and embedded in meaning, and what we seek to know emerges through the inquiry that attends to purposes and framing, that works actively with issues of power and multiple ways of knowing. There is also the meaning of the world we make, through our enactment of intentions, plans, actions and outcomes.

The act of insight can take many forms. It may come in a technical form. James Watson describes his insight one Saturday morning into how the four forms of nucleotide combined in pairs formed the double helix structure of DNA. It may come in an aesthetic form as a poet or artist is touched by a landscape and who expresses that insight in poetic language or a visual representation in a painting. A sculptor may see the potential for creation in a block of stone. Michelangelo is reported to have said that the Pieta already existed in the block of stone before he carved it. It may come as a mental image that captures a line of thought or questioning and which enables a clarity to emerge to lead to further exploration or discussion, as when we say "It dawned me." As we explored in Chapter 2, collaborative inquiry engages many forms of knowing. The study of technical data, such as financial statements and technological reports, involves the application of a scientific or theoretical understanding of the content of these documents. Coming to judgment as to the progress of the partners working together draws on knowledge of relational dynamics. Envisioning a desired future and framing generative images that express the future or the project in metaphorical or allegorical terms draws on a presentational form of knowing. Indeed, it is a valuable process in collaborative inquiry that participants engage in generative imaging or social dreaming, as it is sometimes called, and so enables the group to be creative in expressing its vision for the organization in addressing the issues that the collaborative inquiry was formed to address. We saw this in the vignette in Chapter 1.

Abductive Reasoning

In discussing human knowing, the American philosopher, Charles Peirce describes three forms of reasoning: deductive, inductive and abductive. Deductive reasoning draws on generalizable theory to craft particular arguments whereas inductive reasoning proceeds from particular observations to clarify more generalizable theory. While deductive arguments rest on an internal, logically valid structure with or without evidence, inductive reasoning generates probable conclusions, often basing generalizations on evidence accumulated from various investigations. Abductive reasoning produces exploratory hypotheses. As Peirce

(1903: 230) summarizes, "Deduction proves that something *must* be; induction shows that something *actually is operative*; abduction merely suggests that something *may be.*"

Peirce's three forms of reasoning may be located in the structure of human cognition. Induction and abduction correspond to the direct and reflective insight as answers to questions for intelligence and judgment. They answer different kinds of questions – those that search to pose a question, those that search for an answer, and those that seek to confirm that an answer is true or that it fits the evidence. Deductive reasoning occurs at the operation of understanding, answering the question, What is it? Inductive reasoning, rooted in the evidence, evaluates understanding and pronounces the truth or falsity in the light of experimental testing, just as reflective insights result in a judgment of the adequacy or inadequacy of a provisional understanding, answering the question, Is it so? or How do I know? Abductive reasoning yields plausible explanations about puzzling phenomena and so it accords with the operation of insight into an experience following a question such as, What is going on?

Abductive reasoning occurs in the present tense and is activated by surprise in the face of anomalies or puzzles as they are experienced. In Peirce's view, abduction is the foundation of any new idea and the understanding of any phenomenon. It marks a first step in theory building by abductively conceiving the germ of an idea, an explanation that someday may become a theory, however half-baked that idea may be at a given moment. Without the abductively derived insight, there is no process for development to knowing.

In Peirce's terms, collaborative inquiry participants are engaging in abductive reasoning as they are trying to understand what is going on in the dynamics of the organization and in the inquiry itself. In inquiring in the present tense to generate practical knowing as it occurs in collaborative inquiry, abductive reasoning is essential as organization development and change (ODC) researchers and organizational members are confronted with an array of data. They are typically confronted with surprising and unexpected apparently contradictory and puzzling data in, for example, the interchange of the formalized structures and policies or espoused theory with the learned assumptions or defensive routines of the system (Argyris, 2010; Schein & Schein, 2017). As they question what they see and hear, and question their own questioning, they are inquiring into both the facts of the data sense of what they see and hear and the data of consciousness of their cognitive operations in being attentive, intelligent, reasonable and responsible. Whatever answers they come up with are provisional, what we might call "working hypotheses," until they have been tested.

As Coghlan (2009) demonstrates, ODC researchers subject their experiences and those of the organizational members with whom they are interacting to inquiry in order to search for insight or understanding into their experience. Insights or understanding are then subjected to further inquiry, the outcome of which may lead to inquiry into actions, possibly into goals and into intentionality in order to uncover reasoning behind actions. Any insight generated must be subjected to some sort of shared sense-making, as the participants reflect on how each insight has illuminated inquiry and they check that their insights are reasonable in fitting the evidence. Lastly, the question of appropriate action accompanies the judgment of value as to what is judged to be good to do. This process of shared inquiry is engaged in through exploratory, diagnostic and confrontive questioning (Coghlan, 2009; Schein, 2013).

THE GENERAL EMPIRICAL METHOD

The operations of experience, understanding, judgment and decision/ acting form a general empirical method, which requires

- *Be attentive* to the data
- *Be intelligent* in envisaging possible explanations of that data
- *Be rational* in preferring as probable or certain the explanations which provide the best account for the data
- *Be responsible* for deliberating, deciding and taking acting (Coghlan, 2010).

The general empirical method underpins the specific modes of inquiry across the natural sciences, critical scholarship, social science and practical living in asking intelligent questions about experience and providing and verifying reasonable answers to those questions (Table 3.1). The general empirical method of being attentive, intelligent, reasonable and responsible is a normative pattern of recurring and interrelated activities. It envisages data of sense and of consciousness. It doesn't examine objects without taking into consideration the operations of experience, understanding and judgment. It enables us to appropriate our own conscious reality as existential subjects. It provides a key to the relationship between questioning and answering; it is a framework for collaborative creativity that deals with different kinds of questions, each with its own

Table 3.1   *The structure of human knowing and doing*

Operations of Human Knowing	Levels of Consciousness	Activity	General Empirical Method
Experience	Empirical Level	Attentiveness [to data of sense and of consciousness]	Be attentive
Understanding	Intellectual Level	Intelligence [envisaging possible explanations of that data]	Be intelligent
Judgment	Rational Level	Reasonableness [preferring as probable or certain the explanations which provide the best account for the data]	Be reasonable
Action	Responsible Level	Responsibility [for action]	Be responsible

focus. Questions for understanding specific data (What is happening here?) have a different focus from questions for reflection (Does this fit?) or from questions of responsibility (What ought we to do?). As conscious subjects we can attend to what is going on, both inside and outside ourselves, inquire intelligently, judge reasonably and decide freely and act responsibly. As conscious existential subjects we can accept and confront the fact that it is up to us to decide that our actions will be responsible, that our judgments be reasonable and our investigations intelligent.

Knowing how we know, i.e., being aware that knowing comprises operations of experience, understanding and judgment, is crucial in collaborative inquiry (Coghlan, 2017). Co-inquiry into what participants have experienced, into how they have understood their experience, and into how they have made judgments, is a fruitful approach. Debates about positions and answers, of themselves, are likely to be incomplete and fractious. At the heart of collaborative inquiry is articulation by the participants of how they have come to interpret events and make value judgments, how they have weighed options in making concrete choices, and how they have decided what action to take.

Several further points need to be made. The domains in which knowing occurs in collaborative inquiry settings are multiple and varied. In the realm of technical knowing, insights and judgments may be directed to patterns of scientific and technical data. Insights and judgments into human relationships come through words and gestures as participants engage with each other in teams and other relational settings. In each of these realms the operations of human knowing are invariant, but how they process insights differs. The expression of insight is not always purely cognitive, and it may be difficult to articulate what they have come to understand. The second point is that participants in collaborative inquiry need to attend to the social dynamics of knowing. When they engage in social interaction, the insights of individuals are tested against the insights of others. Then conversation ensues so that shared understanding may be developed and negotiated. This may succeed; or it may not and no shared understanding results. The third point to note is that the processing of insights takes place in the present tense. While the experience in question may have occurred in the past, the questioning and reception of insight occurs in the present. Hence it is imperative to be attentive to how they are questioning and processing insight in the here-and-now so that they do not fall victim to bias, defensive reasoning, or various forms of cognitive distortions (Argyris, 2010).

Any general empirical method works not only within the consciousness of a single individual but with the engagement of conscious individuals with other conscious individuals. Here they encounter the tension of opposites in the experiences, understanding, judgments, decisions and actions of different individuals and groups. Collaborative inquiry is where conscious individuals engage with others to understand their experiences, understanding, judgments, decisions and actions in a mutual, collaborative manner and to come to a new position. Participants may inquire into the experiences of others, the insights they have into those experiences and the meanings they attribute to them, the judgments they have made and the consequent actions they have taken (Coghlan, 2017). Co-inquiry into what participants have experienced and how they have understood, provides a fruitful approach to developing shared understanding, judgments and planned actions. We now develop this point in more detail.

THE PROCESS OF COLLABORATIVE INQUIRY

The collaborative inquiry process is an emergent process that unfolds in the present tense. Dialogue and conversations between the effort partners serve as the cornerstone of the discovery process. Drawing on Schein's (2013) typology of helpful conversation, the dialogic process within collaborative inquiry can work with the knowing processes of the participants. Schein describes several types of inquiry. His first category is *exploratory inquiry*. This is where experience is elicited by generating the story of what has and is taking place in the organization. His second type of inquiry is *diagnostic inquiry*, in which understanding is elicited by exploring how the experience is understood and what causal inter-pretations are being made. His third type of inquiry is *confrontational inquiry*, where the conversation moves to a more explicit sharing of different ideas that new perspectives have generated. Schein argues that if sufficient time is not devoted to exploratory and diagnostic inquiry, confrontational inquiry closes down the conversation and traps the par-ticipants in dependence and debate.

To explore how dialogue works within the frameworks of human knowing let us look at what happens within participants and between participants in a dialogue.

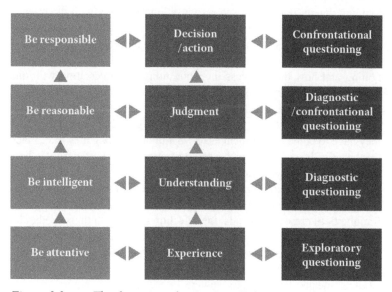

Figure 3.2   The dynamics of enacting collaborative inquiry

Figure 3.2 illustrates the dynamics of collaborative inquiry. At the center are the operations of human knowing: experiencing, understanding, judging and deciding/taking action. On the left-hand side is the enactment of the general empirical method: be attentive to experience, be intelligent in understanding, be reasonable in judging and be responsible in deciding and taking action. On the right-hand side is the form of questioning that enables participants in a collaborative setting to inquire into the experiencing, understanding, judging and deciding/taking action of the others. Exploratory questioning draws out experience. Diagnostic questioning draws out understanding, judging and deciding, while confrontational questioning draws out critical thinking by posing alternatives. The participants are practitioners and researchers. Each draws on its own perspective or community of practice to question and frame its understanding of what is taking place (experience) and its judgment on that understanding, and in then judging what needs to be done. The collaborative engagement brings these perspectives together and by means of exploratory, diagnostic and confrontational questioning in a spirit of humble inquiry may enable the experience, understanding and judgments to be explored. Holding the whole framework together and being attentive, intelligent, reasonable and responsible in working with the process enables the experiences, understandings, judgments and decision/actions of academic and practitioner participants to be respectfully questioned.

Participants in collaborative inquiry need to reflect on their questioning and how they process their questions in conversation with one another and how they subject their knowing to self- and mutual critique. They address the subjectivity–objectivity issue through describing concrete experiences, sharing their emergent insights and articulating how they have to come to judgment as to what understanding they have made that best fits the evidence and by demonstrating critical reflexivity in how they came to judgment (Coghlan, 2017).

Collaborative inquiry in the context of ODC implies efforts which include the active engagement of practitioners and researchers in the framing of the research agenda, the selection and pursuit of methods, and the development of actionable implications. It requires shared inquiry, the joint pursuit of answers to questions of mutual interest through conversation, experimentation, the review and integration of knowledge, or other means. Practitioners engage in collaborative inquiry in order to understand a certain issue or phenomenon using scientifically valid knowledge creation methods. Similarly, researchers engage in collective inquiry in order to understand a certain issue or phenomenon using the collaborative process with practitioners of new knowledge creation. Collaboration does not impose the requirement of an equal partnership in each of these activities, although we posit that a more equal partnership better supports the fulfillment of ODC multiple objectives.

Participants in collaborative inquiry use their experience, understanding and judgment in order to come to know the mixture of experience, understanding, judgment, decisions and actions in the organization that they are studying and helping to change. They make value judgments and decisions as to what interventions might be made. The general empirical method is invariably operative whenever and wherever people ask intelligent questions of experience and thoughtfully assent to reasonable answers. By using the general empirical method, scholar-practitioners can attend to data, think a matter through, and ask the relevant questions. They can know when they have reached reasonable conclusions and can take responsibility for those conclusions. While they can make mistakes, they can also reflect and discover them. Then they can investigate the source of their misunderstandings and false judgments, how they did not attend to all the data or how they jumped to conclusions. They can learn to recognize their biases, prejudices, fears and anxieties. In collaborative research settings, both scholars and practitioners can recognize and question each other's experience, understanding, judgments and actions.

In the vignette described in Chapter 1, the members of the steering group and the two study groups engaged in collaborative inquiry in their separate and joint meetings. In the initial stages of the project the external researchers inquired into the experiences of the insider members. In the early meetings, *exploratory* interventions dominated as the external researchers sought to understand the insider experiences of the members over the previous decade and the members experienced the different understandings among themselves. These understandings were put to the test as the interviews were conducted and answers were codified and analyzed. Then *diagnostic* questioning came more into play as the meanings of the raw data were sought. The answers from the initial interviews were provisional, and in terms of abductive reasoning, they needed to be explored further. The move from the initial interviews of a small group of employees to a more extensive range was the consequence of the abductive reasoning at that point. Further exploratory and diagnostic questioning followed through the invitation to contribute a phrase and the creation of generative imagery through the collages.

The general empirical method was employed throughout as both the external researchers and insider organizational members engaged in exploratory and diagnostic questioning, first to hear the experiences of the organization and second to come to common understanding of what the diverse experiences meant. Reaching common understanding was supported by the application of the scientific analytic tools of data analysis which were then taken to the realm of the generative imagery. All through the meetings and interviews the participants sought to be attentive to experience, intelligent in understanding, and reasonable in making judgments which formed the basis for the action stages of the project. Throughout, the external researchers acted as engaged scholarship in the manner of Mode 2 knowledge production, by listening, supporting, questioning, providing theory (e.g., on capabilities when appropriate), overseeing the structure, providing the technical expertise in codifying and analyzing the data, and facilitating the sense-making.

MODALITIES OF COLLABORATIVE INQUIRY

Collaborative inquiry is a generalized term and is used to refer to a family of approaches or modalities. Coghlan (2010) has provided a way of delineating these modalities in terms of generative insights that give each modality its own distinctive character and emphasis, and how the general empirical method may be applied within that character. By generative insight, Coghlan means an insight by the person or group that first constructed it that was foundational in framing that modality and which led to the development of further insights and methods of working within each modality. Some of the different modalities include action learning, appreciative inquiry, clinical inquiry, cooperative inquiry, intervention research and learning history, to name some common ones.

Schein's (1987) insight was that adopting a clinical stance whereby an organization's pathologies are identified, clinical interventions are made to enable the healthy functioning of the organization. In contrast, Cooperrider's (2017) generative insight was that in every organization something works somewhere, so a focus on asking appreciative questions enables people to think in new ways which may lead to acting in new ways. From this insight, appreciative inquiry emerged; a cycle of four Ds (Discovery, Dream, Design and Delivery) to enable researchers and practitioners to move from experience to selected action and to attend to and receive insights to understand the power of positive questioning. Revans' (1998) generative insights were, "There can be no learning without action and no (sober and deliberate) action without learning" (p. 83) and "Those unable to change themselves cannot change what goes on around them" (p. 85). From these insights he framed action learning. Heron and Reason's (2008) insight of a group process whereby the participants work together in an inquiry group as co-researchers and co-subjects framed the essence of cooperative inquiry. The generative insight underpinning the learning history approach is that rather than presenting the univocal voice of a single author or group of researchers, a learning history presents concurrent, multiple and often divergent voices in an organizational story (Bradbury & Mainmelis, 2001). Presenting the jointly told tale is enabled by the format, whereby columns of narrative text are juxtaposed with the interpretative voice of participants (often disagreeing) and the voice of the learning historian. Hearing and reading the multiple voices and perspectives within the process of a learning history enable insight into the insights of others and through conversation the possibilities for new shared insights to emerge, on which judgments may be reached and actions planned and taken.

We are not devoting space to elaborating on these modalities. These are done elsewhere (e.g., Coghlan 2010; Bradbury 2015). The point we are making is that the modalities, such as captured above, are situated within the Mode 2 knowledge creation cluster and illustrate somewhat different inquiry emphasis. All are grounded in a world view of partnership and collaboration around issues that matter to whatever constituencies are involved and aim to generate actionable knowledge.

ETHICAL CHALLENGES IN COLLABORATIVE INQUIRY

Ethics are an integral component of all social science research (Kaplan, 1964). At the most basic level, ". . . to be ethical is to conform to accepted professional practices . . ." (Bailey, 1978: 381). We have been arguing that collaborative inquiry is grounded in a philosophy of practical knowing which focuses on the everyday actions of organizations. As we have explored in Chapter 2 and in this chapter, practical action is driven by a series of choices people make in deciding what to do – choices which are grounded in assessments about what they judge to be worthwhile and valuable as they ask what courses of action are open to them, how they review and weigh options, reach decisions, and choose to act. The starting point of our approach is that ethics are not a set of rules or a calculus of risks and benefits, but rather the embodiment of the intelligent, reasonable and responsible selves that participants try to enact in the collaborative inquiry process.

In traditional Mode 1 research settings, researchers and participants engage at a single point of contact, namely the researcher's agenda, to obtain information from the participant. In this one-sided relationship the ethical issues that arise typically focus on doing good, not doing harm and respecting the person. In collaborative inquiry the external researchers and organizational members engage in a partnership in selecting the questions, planning and implementing the research and processing the results. As collaborative inquiry takes place in the present tense and has an emergent unfolding nature, as it attempts to integrate inquiry with everyday organizational action, one may argue that the ethical issues are not different from those of living a good life. Collaborative inquiry can be an ethics praxis method as it combines three values (Nielsen, 2017). It joins ethics with actionable learning. It helps make the actor and the world developmentally better and it uses inductive, practitioner-based theory building that is helpful for both practitioners and academics.

We suggest three ethical questions which the researchers and participants need to be clear about, discuss and agree the answers.

1. If researchers and participants collaborate closely, how can confidentiality and anonymity be preserved? As collaborative inquiry is a political enterprise and has consequences for the participants and researchers, it is difficult to guarantee anonymity and confidentiality, as others can easily know who participated and may be able to identify who said or contributed what.
2. If collaborative inquiry takes place in the present tense and is emergent, how can informed consent be meaningful? Neither researchers nor participants can know in advance where the process will take them and cannot know to what they are consenting. As a change process can create its own resistance, researchers or participants cannot be expected to withdraw in the face of opposition (albeit by small groups within the project).
3. As collaborative inquiry can have political consequences, how can the researchers avoid doing harm to participants? We suggest two ways of answering this question: the establishment of ethical ground rules for the project and the extent to which the collaboration and negotiation occurs, so that participants own the findings as much as the researcher.

CONCLUSIONS

This chapter has introduced a method for engaging in collaborative inquiry. As Coghlan (2010) discusses, a method is not the same as a recipe, which produces another instance of the same dish. A method, rather, provides a key to the relationship between questioning and answering. As the contemporary natural sciences are characterized by the methods in their respective fields, so the general empirical method – embedded in the Mode 2 orientation and inquiring in the present tense to create practical knowledge – described in this chapter provides a method for working in the social science of organization development (Coghlan et al., 2019). In the collaborative context, the general empirical method is a framework for engaging with the different meanings that the participants may hold about their experience. The benefits of this approach are that it situates inquiry within ordinary human knowing that follows abductive logic. It situates participants non-hierarchically with other inquirers. It provides a touchstone from which inquiry can proceed collaboratively by providing a cognitional structure within which each participant operates differently that makes collaborative inquiry. Accordingly, what becomes pivotal for the success of such collaboration is the creation and utilization of a space for dialogue among the members of a community of practice (the practitioner and researchers) to form a community of inquiry in order to improve a system's performance and to add to the broader body of knowledge in the field of management and organizations.

4.   Transformation and design

In Chapter 1 we presented the essence of collaborative inquiry for organization development and change (ODC). Chapter 2 provided the theoretical underpinning and the philosophical orientation of the social science in organization development (OD), the key features of knowledge creation, Mode 1, Mode 2 and generative change orientations. In Chapter 3 we established the method of engaging in collaborative inquiry as grounded in the operations of human knowing in terms of a general empirical method: be attentive to experience, be intelligent in understanding, be reasonable in making judgments and be responsible in taking action. We brought the mindset, methodology, methods and variety of collaborative inquiry orientations to the forefront. This chapter explores the essence of transformation, transformation process and design orientations that are the foundation of collaborative inquiry. Figure 4.1 captures the key elements of transformation and design.

COLLABORATIVE TRANSFORMATIONAL CHANGE ORIENTATION

As we have seen, collaborative inquiry is an emergent change process within a complex adaptive system that aims at developing partnership in the process of new knowledge creation. As such, by its very nature it is a transformational endeavor. Transformational change implies radical change in the organization's identity, how the organization functions and how members of the organization perceive, think and behave (Bartunek & Louis, 1988). It is viewed as a process that leads to the "... emergence of a new state, unknown until it takes place/shape, out of the remains of a chaotic death of the old state were the time period for the change process in not easily controlled ..." (Ackerman & Anderson, 2001: 3). It entails second-order change that includes changes in the organization's mission and identity that trigger an organizational redesign of the way the organization works (Bartunek & Jones, 2017). It is considered as a "holistic" rather than a "limited" or a "focused" approach to change (Mitki et al., 2000). It is viewed as a "guided changing" rather than a

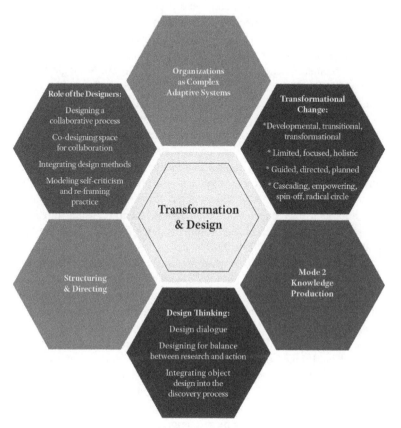

Figure 4.1   Collaborative inquiry: transformation and design

"directed" or "planned" change orientation (Buono & Kerber, 2008). Lastly, it is considered as one of the three main clusters of organization development of change orientations, the others being "developmental" and "transitional" (Ackerman & Anderson, 2001).

One primary division among organizational transformation perspectives is the concept of planned versus emergent change. Planned change is a "formal procedure that is introduced and actively managed by managers or consultants" and participation for organization members is "typically expected to occur within the framework of the designed change" (Livne-Tarandach & Bartunek, 2009: 4). The assumption that organizational transformation can be intentional and executed in orderly, clearly delineated sequential steps and a predictable fashion underlies the planned change perspective (Greenbaum et al., 2020). Examples of planned change approaches to organization transformation include the Flow of Change (Kotter, 1996; Kotter and Cohen, 2002); Sociotechnical System Planned Change (STS) (Pasmore et al., 2019); Strategic Fitness Process (SFP) (Beer, 2020); Information Processing (Galbraith, 1995); and Built to Change (B2C) (Lawler & Worley, 2011).

An alternative perspective is that of emergent change, which asserts that organizational change is "continuous, unpredictable, and essentially political in nature" (Livne-Tarandach & Bartunek, 2009: 5). Given the inability to plan fully and control the change process from the top, the emergent change perspective often arises from a wide variety of areas and organizational levels. Scholars assert that the success of the emergent approach may depend on organizations facing constant threats in "dynamic and unpredictable environments to which they constantly have to adapt" (Todnem By, 2005: 376).

One perspective is that transformational change may more effectively originate from the individuals within an organization (more of a bottom-up or middle-out perspective), rather than from a proscribed direction from the organization's leaders (a top-down approach) or outside experts (Beer, 2020). In their recent examination of the evolution of organizational transformation and organization development, Bartunek and Jones explain that "adequate attention is not explicitly paid to the experiences of individuals being exposed and participating in particular change processes" (2017: 144). Bartunek and Jones also indicate that examining individuals' participation in organizational transformation can provide a more comprehensive understanding of the transformation process or the "guided changing" orientation that Buono and Kerber (2008) describe.

As was argued earlier, another area of emphasis relates to the level of individual engagement in the transformation process. Individuals' cognitive mindsets are likely to influence both the transformation process and its outcomes. Framing, frames of references and interpretive schemas all play a role (Bartunek, 1984; Jorgenson & Steier, 2013; Maxton & Bushe, 2018). Schemas – viewed as world views or frames of reference or mental frameworks – held by individual members impact the way that information is allowed in, organized and perceived, and the way organizational members act (Bruning, 1994; Bartunek, 1984). Creating the space for the sharing of individual frames of references and interpretive schemas are important in the enhancement of individual appreciations of one another and in the formation of shared interpretive schemas that are one of the early steps in the formation of new collective mindsets that impact transformation.

A few common denominators between the different perspectives of organization transformation stand out: (1) they can start at different company levels with diverse interests and agendas, i.e., "limited," or "focused" or "holistic" change; (2) all tend to be of an emergent nature; (3) all organization transformation involves new and old forums of collaboration between members of the organizations and members from outside the organization (researchers or consultants); (4) all involve a form of partnership between the actors involved; (5) all involve a high level of shared commitment and engagement; (6) all involve changing individual mindsets and the creation of shared collective schemas; and (7) all are based on collective new meaning creation or sense making (Shani et al., 2018). For example, in the vignette presented in Chapter 1, the early intent or focus was to address the issue of a potential threat of limited change capabilities. The goal was not to transform the organization. The emergent nature of the project, the collaboration and partnership in the discovery phase, the high level of engagement of members of the organization in the sharing of learning and the new insights generated, resulted in a system transformation that included new ways of thinking, new ways of organizing, new work processes and roles, and new working relationships.

The emergent quality nature of organization transformation has led to the identification of a number of organizational transformation processes (Bartunek & Jones, 2017; Pasmore, 2015; Romanelli & Tushman, 1994; Wischnevsky & Damanpour, 2006). These studies assert that any process of organizational transformation requires involvement at different levels of an organization, both in terms of leadership and engagement of employees. Yet, there may be significant differences in the dynamics of the process that explain which learning mechanisms are best suited to address rapid transitions in the context. Following Greenbaum et al. (2020), four approaches to organizational transformation have been identified. The approaches are explored along two dimensions, activation and institutionalization, and are captured in Figure 4.2. The two fundamental dimensions used are activation and institutionalization:

- Who *activates* the transformation process, i.e., whether the perception of the need to change and the ignition of the change process comes from the top of the firm or the bottom;

- Who *institutionalizes* the change, i.e., whether the formalization of the change process into the organization and the management of the change process once it is institutionalized comes from the top or the bottom.

		Activation	
		Top	**Bottom**
Institutionalization	**Top**	Cascading	Radical Circle
	Bottom	Empowering	Spin-off

Source: Adapted (with minor modifications) from Greenbaum et al. (2020).

Figure 4.2   *Organizational transformation orientation: institutionalizing and activation forces*

The common denominator of all four approaches is that each either develops or enhances a unique tapestry of learning mechanism that guides and at times carries out the transformation. The first category of the organizational transformation forces is *cascading*: change activated from the top and institutionalized from the top. Organizations may be facing increasing pressure on performance in a stable environment and seek targeted organizational improvement. In a more stable environment, change is likely activated by top executives, as they may be in the best position to perceive a need for change. The change process is then institutionalized into a collaborative inquiry initiative and process that is cascaded down to the firm. Participation is often appointed by leadership and the targeted outcomes of this process are most often new organizational insights and improvement.

One example of this collaborative inquiry process can be seen in a semiconductor company's transformation process. In this case the collaborative inquiry project was driven by the perceived and anticipated future competition and thus the need to improve both innovation and efficiency. The initiative was a top-down-driven transformation that was viewed as essential for the future of the company's survival. The company was doing well by all performance indicators. A parallel learning structure composed of a steering committee, a study group and an ideas committee were established to lead and carry out the project. It is called a parallel learning structure as it is parallel to the existing organizational structures (Bushe & Shani, 1991). We will develop the notion of parallel learning structures in the process of change in Chapter 5. The top executive team was actively involved in the process at every step. A wide variety of ideas was generated as a result of the discovery process and ongoing dialogue. Some of the changes that were implemented included a major restructuring of the company, key R&D processes and restructuring of the manufacturing process (for more details, see Shani & Elliott, 1998; Bushe & Shani, 1991).

The second category of the organizational forces is *empowering*. Companies may be seeking company-wide incremental change. The activation process is still initiated by top executives, but the orchestration of the process is greatly diffused to the bottom of the organization – institutionalization of the change process is dependent on input and leadership from lower levels of the organization. Ultimately, firms may be seeking culture change and empowering employees to contribute creatively to that process may be highly effective.

An example of such an orientation is the case of a collaborative inquiry initiative with a large pharmacy division of a health maintenance organization (HMO). The pharmacy division operated as a semi-autonomous organization and was organized on a geographic or self-contained basis, had four levels of management organization and included 50 individual clinic pharmacies. The project was initiated by top executives, but the orchestration of the project and process was such that it would engage the bottom level in both the discovery and implementation of the changes. A communication forum that included a steering committee and a communication study team that included 15 individuals was established to lead and carry out the study. The executive committee wanted to provide input but not necessarily be the decision maker in the discovery process, generations of ideas for change, or implementation of the changes. Many of the ideas were generated by lower levels of the organization that resulted in system-wide transformation, including restructuring of the division, the number and location of pharmacies, redesign of the ordering processes, and interfaces with both customers and suppliers (for more details, see Stebbins & Shani, 1989a, 1989b, 2009).

Similarly, an electronic company in the telecommunication industry experienced increasing market pressures that forced the company to rethink the development of new product processes and how to sustain change capabilities. The project was initiated by the executive team, established a tapestry of learning mechanisms that included a steering committee and a task force, and followed an emergent transformation process guided by an SFP to incorporate and enhance organizational dialogue and action. The project resulted in a wide range of outcomes including a new organization strategy, new product development processes, a restructuring of the organization, new ways of communication, institutionalization of both the SFP process and the learning mechanisms tapestry, a 10% increase of market share and an overall 15% increase in company profit (for more details, see Beer, 2020 and Fredberg et al., 2011).

We identify the *spin-off* as the third category of our organizational transformation matrix. The motivation may likely originate from employee-generated ideas not being supported or aligned with their firm's current or future strategic vision. Participation in this process is essentially predetermined by the make-up of the employee group that generated the rejected idea. The ultimate goal is a decoupling of the idea-generating group of employees from the organization.

By comparison, *radical circles* are activated from the bottom of the organization but institutionalized from the top. The radical circle comprises employees motivated by their question who feel unease with the firm's current strategic vision. The circle aims to disrupt the current strategic direction and could be most effective in generating rapid breakthrough changes in the firm's environment. The transformation at Microsoft to enter the hardware space with the Xbox video game console was driven by a radical circle of four engineers, without any ignition from the top, and well ahead of Microsoft management's recognition of the disruption coming to the firm's competitive environment. However, radical circles eventually rely on institutionalization from the top. Once the radical circle reveals itself, the purpose is not to disrupt and destroy its own organization, but to lead it into a new direction. External experts were brought in to help in the transformation process. The radical circle's proposed change to the organization's strategic vision needs resources and support, and therefore, after the pain and suffering of the quest (the process by which the radical circle refines and further sharpens its alternative strategic vision), top management recognition and endorsement to scale up the initiative is critical for the success chances of the new vision. The engagement and insights of the external researchers is a way to enlarge the circle of engagement throughout the organization in the discovery process. The radical circle in many ways serves as a learning mechanism, in that while it emerges in a natural way, it acts as the facilitator in the development of a new mindset, new shared meaning, and new knowledge creation (for more details, see Verganti & Shani, 2016 and Greenbaum et al., 2020).

The four different clusters of organization transformation orientations – cascading, empowering, spin-off and radical circles (see Figure 4.2) – share in common high levels of engagement, an emphasis on inquiry and learning, the sharing of individual mindsets and creation of collective interpretive schemes, the creation or enhancement of a tapestry of learning mechanisms, and the collective sense-making that results in new knowledge creation. All four transformation orientations share in common partnership with external researchers during the transformation processes, the engagement of the executive teams in the transformation process, and the design orientation that guides the collaborative inquiry process.

THE DESIGN ORIENTATION

Since its conception in the late 1940s and 1950s, the field of organization development has emerged as a hybrid outcome of the emerging practice, theoretical development and careful design and facilitation of different approaches to enhance system improvement efforts. Thus far in this book we have emphasized the emergent quality of collaborative inquiry. Most of the early designers' emphasis and published work was more on the "action" and less on the "research" component of the intervention. The collaborative inquiry organization development mindset and orientation strikes the balance between action and research by its design.

One of the paradoxes in the field of ODC is that a design perspective tends not to be an area of emphasis even though most ODC interventions while also based in emergent social processes tend to be purposefully designed and managed. When we think of design and designers, we can identify three broad perspectives. The first – the traditional – is styling: designers are asked to design a product or a process or an interface that can be sold to others which are likely to find it appealing (e.g., for its shape, color, attractiveness). The second is user-centered: designers get closer to users, discover their needs, values and priorities, and then generate a creatively wide variety of possible ideas. The third – system designers – are the designers who possess content and process know-how that follows a specific design theory school of thought with a set of design principles and processes. Some examples of the diverse specific orientations include sociotechnical design principles and planned change process (i.e., Pasmore, 1988); design-driven innovation process (i.e., Press, Verganti et al., 2020; Verganti, 2009); organization design and redesign principles and process (i.e., Galbraith, 1995; MacKenzie, 1986); or strategic fitness design principles and process (Beer, 2020). Each one of the orientations is likely to provide a somewhat different guide to the optimal design or redesign process of the system (Pasmore, 2020; Shani & Stebbins, 1987).

From an ODC perspective, the design process that is crafted and the actual process of creating and implementing it, make a difference (Mohrman & Pillans, 2013; Stebbins & Shani, 1989b). OD scholar-practitioners, embedded in collaborative inquiry practice, utilize the depth and breadth of design and design process-oriented knowledge, and through conversations and dialogue with members of the organization a collective choice is made about the appropriate change and development process to follow. In the vignette that was shared in Chapter 1, the initial designer role was a collaborative effort by the external researchers, the VP for HR and the CEO. The early conversations resulted in the crafting of a tentative road map for a possible project, to be framed and re-framed by the steering group as the project progressed. In the following section of the chapter we explore the role of the co-designers in collaborative inquiry OD, and we examine the historical evolution of design thinking, the influence of collaborative design orientation for the purpose of creating new meaning on system transformation, and the role of the collaborative inquiry designers.

Structuring and Directing

In designing collaborative inquiry, a useful consideration is to distinguish between structuring and directing. Structuring as an intervention refers to *what* designers may do with regard to structuring a project. Structuring may be understood as a continuum from high to medium to low structure. Directing refers to *how* structure may be used along a continuum of imposing it in a directive manner to a non-directive manner in which participants adopt their own program and process (Coughlan & Coghlan, 2011). As Coughlan and Coghlan demonstrate, structuring/ non-structuring and directiveness/non-directiveness may be plotted in relation to one another (Figure 4.3). Point A marks low structuring and low directiveness, point B high structuring and low directiveness, point C low structuring and high directiveness, and point D high structuring and high directiveness. As meetings and other interventions are designed the designers need to deal with the challenges that structuring and directing pose, or, to express it in terms of Figure 4.2, to plot their position on the grid. In designing a group meeting, for example, how much will the agenda and the meeting's process be controlled? How much will participants' views dictate the pace of the meeting? In the context of collaborative inquiry where some structuring is necessary or desirable, how structures are introduced and operated within the collaborative inquiry ODC paradigm is a critical design challenge and may be a source of tension.

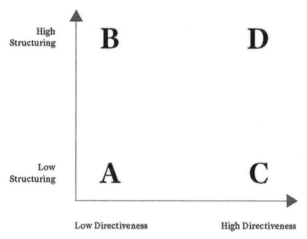

Figure 4.3   *Directiveness and structuring*

Collaborative Inquiry Designers

External researchers in the collaborative inquiry process are usually the ones that bring the know-how about the design of such an endeavor. As has been advanced throughout this book, external researchers may be the trigger of the project design process, or the catalyst, or co-designers with members of the organization. As design is a critical component of collaborative inquiry in OD initiatives, it is important to understand the roots of the design orientation in the study of organization and organization change. Design thinking emerged from the design methods movement of the 1960s. Simon (1996: 9) proposed the science of design as "a body of intellectually tough, analytic, partly formalizable, partly empirical, teachable doctrine about the design process." In capturing the evolution and current state of design methods, Jones (1970) was the first to catalogue the variety of approaches to design, both rational and creative. Subsequent authors continued in this direction; Lawson (2006) is credited with beginning a process of generalizing the concept of design thinking. Design thinking was adapted for business purposes by David Kelley, who founded IDEO in 1991, and has been utilized ever since (see, e.g., Hatchuel, 2005; Martin, 2009; Verganti, 2009; Norman, 2010; Kupp et al., 2017; Press, Bellis et al., 2020).

The design school of thought evolved within the field of organization and management and was influenced by the body of knowledge that emerged in the sociotechnical system design school and the innovation stream that has adopted the form of design thinking. Schön (1983) observed that the design dialogue is a critical trigger for introspection, self-criticism and re-framing. The "talk back" that the designer(s) experience(s) in designing with materials is what inculcates a reflective practitioner. A diverse set of designers – trained or not – need to be self-critical to avoid going in the same direction, whilst seeking a shared direction. As such, design as a discipline is a unique human act, where individuals share their cognitive frames, open to framing and re-framing and work at developing a collective cognitive frame (Jorgenson & Steier, 2013). Such a collective frame tends to guide new meaning creation and interpretations. At the most basic level, the power of design is the ability to empower and engage others in the discovery process. By focusing more on encouraging others to share cognitive mindsets and collectively reflect on it, new meaning is created (Bartunek, 1984). As such, the design process is viewed as an emergent process between participants in a specific context.

As suggested earlier, the quality of the partnership between the members of the organization and the external researchers drives the co-design process and outcome. The collaborative inquiry in organization development and change practice are powerful drivers of change initiative and do not merely supplement methodological thinking and action. The critical question for the collaborative inquiry design, and co-designers, is whether the participants achieve new knowledge through making or creating the new narratives that, if well-designed, will inherently have a new meaning, as it is a social and collective creation. The social integration fundamentally demands that leaders themselves are involved in the process and display a positive force for change. The challenge is that many boundaries exist, increasing the social integration challenge and raising the need for a fundamental shift of our paradigm towards a more dialogical-based perspective and practice (Schön, 1988). For example, in a collaborative inquiry project with a company in the fashion and design industry that focused on the challenge of continuous creativity, the co-designers (which included the researchers, R&D, a VP and a Strategy VP), developed a tentative blueprint for the project as a starting point. Based on the company culture and identity, one of the core ideas was to integrate design thinking into the inquiry process. All the data collection activities involved the creation of a design, flowcharts, graphs, drawings and pictures. Individual creations were shared and the dialogues led both to the development of a new level of appreciation for individuals' ways of thinking and the creation of new shared schemas and understanding beyond the boundaries of the co-designers' understanding of the current and future needs and desires (for more details, see Cirella et al., 2012 and Shani et al., 2012).

Sharing and creating objects within a shared, social space, is the core of design (Friedman et al., 2016). As stated earlier, design objects can range from pictures, collage, sculpture, stories, creating a shared carpet, carpet tiles, sketches, 3-D models and the like. It is where and when both collaborative inquiry scholar-practitioners and members of the organization can establish common ground for collaborative action and transformation. A key to triggering new thinking and insight is the utilization of sketches, metaphors, images, generative images, models, prototypes (and the like), all of which are a part of the design language that acts as a visualization of understandings, influences and intentions (Porter, 1988; Drew & Guillemin, 2014). Goodman (1976: 38) describes the power of visualization: "Talking does not make the world or even pictures, but talking and pictures participate in making each other and the world as we know them." This is what we can see in the vignette in Chapter 1. The imagery and emergent collages shifted the conversation from the scientific mode of knowing through performance data to a presentational form of knowing through the generative imagery that engendered energy and enthusiasm for change.

Schön's observation that "In a design process, each party reveals her view of the object, and perhaps also her interpretation of the other's messages" captures the added value of design and design thinking in the collaborative inquiry process (Schön, 1988: 183). Through enacting the general empirical method of inquiry into experience through exploratory questioning and into understanding through diagnostic questioning the participants can come to understand and appreciate each other's perspective. Thus, through abductive reasoning they can articulate provisional designs which are refined as the project progresses. So long as the parties are jointly committed to making an object, they find it difficult to avoid dealing with their differences of perception and interpretation (Schön, 1988). This perspective offers a key insight into system development and transformation – the co-creation of the design process not only reflects the evolution of the design object, but also the emergence and convergence of collective shared meaning. If this collaborative inquiry dialogue occurs, designing can become an enabler of a system to stimulate change in the designers' mindset, stakeholders and the environment (Pendleton-Jullian & Brown, 2018). As meaning emerges through the iterative co-construction of representations in social situations, they can serve as a catalyst for new ideas, action and, ultimately, individual and system transformation (Press, Bellis et al., 2020). An illustration of the designers' role in the collaborative inquiry project with a biopharma company included external researchers and internal researchers as the project co-designers. The initiative was driven by the need to develop new capabilities and resulted in the sequential co-design and development of three projects, each of which was led by the co-design of a distinct tapestry of learning mechanisms that guided and facilitated the projects (Roth et al., 2008).

The designers of a collaborative inquiry initiative's early engagement with the system is critical in understanding the basic "mess" or needs or desires, and what are the initial requirements, all of which serve as contextual factors. During the early engagement a mutual education takes place, as the designers share their collaborative inquiry and dialogical orientations while the system partners share their insights about the state of the system, its challenges and opportunities. The basic design requirements arrived at through abductive reasoning are viewed as the minimum set of conditions that leaders aim at that the effort (and investment) would achieve (Lillrank et al., 2001). Ideally, through the dialogues, the designers would be able to identify specific requirements based on the nature of the organization and previous experiences with collaborative inquiry-based change initiatives. Next, the designers identify design dimensions that are viewed as the basic set of alternative activities in the change process that leaders can choose from in order to meet the design requirements (Kolodny et al., 2001). Critical to note is that during this early engagement the researchers facilitate the collaborative inquiry dialogue that will allow all the partners to collectively arrive at a shared and agreed-upon set of requirements and dimensions. How the challenges that were provided by the two members of the executive team in the vignette described in Chapter 1 (who shared their disagreements/opposition with both the process and content of what was being advanced) were dealt with, is an example of the power of the collaborative environment. The design requirements that were explored included the extent to which individuals wanted to invest time and energy in the collaborative inquiry project, to what extent individuals felt that the system was ready for such a study that might involve organization transformation, and to what extent the resources, knowledge and skills were available or could be made available.

Another example of design requirements that were a part of the collaborative inquiry project with the fashion and design company that was briefly mentioned earlier included to what extent the executive team was open to redesigning the design teams' work processes, if needed; the extent to which organizational members was agreeable to create new work routines in a non-routine work environment whose identity is creativity; and the extent to which design teams were willing to integrate input from customers, suppliers and manufacturing into the design process. The design perspective in collaborative inquiry projects blended together the collaborative orientation of co-design, the openness to emergent design and redesign process, the integration of object design into the discovery process, and openness to the challenge that rested in the development of shared cognitive and interpretive schemas.

The role of design and designers can also be demonstrated by examination of a project that was carried out with a company that served mostly the defense industry. The collaborative inquiry project was initiated by the executive team that was concerned about potential budget cuts. The secrecy-based culture required high level of commitment across the executive team and active involvement in co-designing of the project. A wide variety of barriers evolved as the project progressed, such as the "need-to-know" culture and real silos between product unities. The project resulted in the development of shared cognitive understanding of the organization by the study team and steering committee, and a comprehensive set of recommendation for a re-design of the company, its key processes, and the re-thinking of HR practices. Yet, due to the complexity of the company context, managers and organization members that were not actively involved in the discovery process had a hard time accepting what was presented. Coupling this with the turnaround of the industry (the budget cuts that were anticipated did not materialize and additional resources were provided) resulted in shelving the recommendations (Stebbins et al., 2006). While the external environment shift and distinct and rigid company culture generated great learning opportunities, new shared understandings and new discoveries for those involved, it did not result in the initially desired goal of company transformation.

CONCLUSIONS

Having captured the essence of collaborative inquiry for organization development (Chapter 1), reviewed the theoretical underpinning and the philosophical orientation of the social science in organization development, the essence of knowledge creation, Mode 1, Mode 2 and generative change orientations (Chapter 2), and examined methods of collaborative inquiry (Chapter 3), this chapter has focused on transformation and design orientation. This chapter has magnified the essence of organization transformation and its conceptual foundation, and argued that collaborative inquiry by its very nature triggers such transformation. We have explored how collaborative inquiry design orientation is crucial in providing a structural context for the engagement of all parties in the collaborative endeavor. Both design and transformation play a critical role in the emergence and implementation of the change process. In the next chapter we describe the phases through which the design and implementation of a collaborative inquiry moves.

5.   Phases, mechanisms and quality

The field of organization development and change, since its conception in the late 1940s and 1950s, emerged as a hybrid result of the emerging practice, theoretical development and careful design and facilitation of different approaches to enhance system improvement efforts. Thus far in this volume we have emphasized the emergent quality of collaborative inquiry. Most of the early "designers" and "transformation" emphasis and published work was more on the "action" and less on the "research" component of the intervention. As we have seen in Chapter 4, the collaborative inquiry organization development mindset and orientation strikes the balance between action and research by design. This chapter, focusing on the collaborative inquiry phases and mechanisms challenge, explores the research rigor, relevance and reflective components of collaborative inquiry in organization development practice. We advance a generic change process and mechanisms with six phases. We further explore the design choices – of research orientation, methodologies and tools – available to designers in the co-framing of the overall collaborative inquiry organization development initiative and some of the choices available within each of the phases. Critical emphasis is given to the implications for enhancing relevance, rigor and reflective practice (Pasmore et al., 2008; Rajagopalan, 2020).

Collaborative inquiry as a transformation process can meet the triple goals of being rigorous, reflective and relevant. As can be seen throughout this book, collaborative inquiry also requires effective co-design and facilitation that appreciate the need to orchestrate a complex agile change and development initiative. As we have seen in Chapter 4, leading an organization transformation process is not a simple endeavor and tends to consume significant resources and commitment, and requires openness to learning with high levels of engagement.

COLLABORATIVE INQUIRY PHASES AND MECHANISMS

One of the key objectives of collaborative inquiry, as we have argued in Chapters 2 and 3, is to generate new knowledge. While all inquiry tries to understand something important through means that limit the likelihood of working from false insights, the collaborative process foundation can be seen as an important methodology that generates new and useful knowledge. The collaborative nature of the inquiry process and its dialogical-based foundation is aided by the establishment of learning mechanisms that provide a platform for the integration of multiple perspectives, enable discoveries, and which tend to trigger mind shifts, the development of new mindsets and new meaning creation.

Placing collaborative inquiry within the broad paradigm of social science research, we have advocated in Chapters 1 and 2 that the key elements of this approach suggest a best fit within the Mode 2 knowledge production cluster. Research with living systems and most human inquiry processes, by their very nature, follows specific steps in order to meet basic knowledge creation (e.g., Reason, 1988; Mohrman et al., 2011; Van de Ven, 2011). Collaborative inquiry, as we have seen in this book, is an emergent process that unfolds in the present tense. As such, we identify six generic inquiry phases that seem to be implemented in one variation or another in collaborative inquiry organization development and change projects. The six phases and their sequence need to be viewed as a place from which to start as most clients and researchers would want to craft a possible roadmap. Furthermore, we view the process as a composite of phases and not sequential steps. The critical point to emphasize is that each project emerges somewhat differently based on the distinct business context, the dynamics of the organization and the dynamics of the relationship with the researchers.

PHASES OF COLLABORATIVE INQUIRY

The generic phases of collaborative inquiry for organization development draw on the work of Coghlan et al. (2019), Guerci et al. (2019), Shani et al. (2020), the review of published organization development (OD) research and the authors' experience in the field for a combined 60 years. Figure 5.1 summarizes the phases in the framework:

0. Initial conversations between an organization and researchers about a possible collaborative project.
1. Initial framing and co-framing of the project scope around real organization issues or challenges.
2. Collaborative exploration of the organization's context and the Mode 2 research orientation with key members of the system.
3. Collaborative re-framing of the project purpose, scope, the research question/s, framing of the inquiry type, collaborative exploration of research methodology and the design of collaborative spaces.
4. Collaborative inquiry process that is embedded in data collection, the development and capturing of systemic narratives, generative images, meaning creation, the design and facilitation of the data sense-making process and continuous experimentation within the collaborative spaces.
5. Execution of the changes and the dissemination of the newly created knowledge in academic and professional outlets.

Phase 0 – Preliminary Conversation about a Possible Collaborative Project

The starting point is when the organization experiences some disruption of the status quo and a need for change. The stimulus is most likely to come from the external VUCA (volatile, uncertain, complex, ambiguous) environment but it can also come from within, as instanced in the vignette in Chapter 1, where, from her MBA course, Mia noticed some emerging industry-based challenges and the potential of her company to engage in a collaborative inquiry venture in order to be one step ahead of the competition. An organization's management needs to find external researchers who can be of help. Here, the choice to go down the route of collaborative inquiry rather than the more traditional "doctor–patient" consulting firm route is paramount.

Once that decision has been made, preliminary exchanges between researchers and contact organization members take place. These initial conversations are critical as beyond arriving at a go/not-go decision for the initial framing of a possible project and its scope, both parties need to gauge the possible added value and to what extent such a project can address their respective needs. In this phase, the parties are engaged in

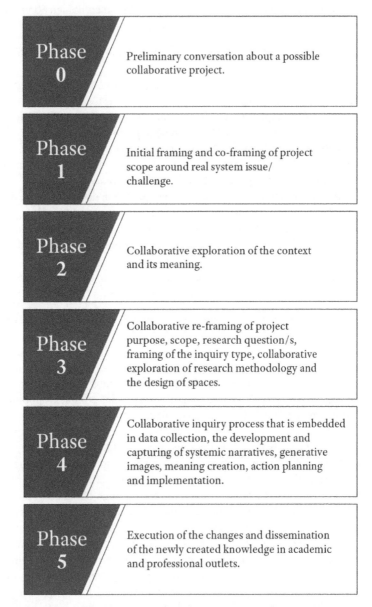

Figure 5.1   Phases in collaborative inquiry

a preliminary mutual education process as they learn about one another and assess if both parties are ready to jointly undertake a collaborative inquiry project. This set of initial conversations can also serve as an opportunity to have humble conversations, share mutual expectations, the essence of the potential partnership and its meaning, the nature of the emergent process and possible generic phases. Such conversations set in motion the foundation for partnership, collaboration and continuous learning.

Phase 1 – Initial Framing and Co-framing of Project Scope Around a Real System Issue/Challenge

Having agreed to proceed, the organization's management and the external researchers begin to explore the reasons for initiating the change and development project. These conversations usually result in an initial framing or co-framing of the project and its scope around a provisional identification of needs and/or challenges facing the organization. The essence of the conversations and mutual education that take place during this phase among possible project partners allows for the beginning of the establishment of working relationships as individuals get to know one another and begin to appreciate the potential added value of each other and the potential added value to the organization for a possible project. The insiders provide a broad review of the organization and its internal and external context – its past, its present and possible future challenges – and possible motives for the change and development effort, while the external researchers provide further pre-review of the collaborative inquiry orientation and the nature of its emergent process quality within organization development practice.

The researchers utilize humble inquiry through the general empirical method by *exploratory* questioning to hear the experience of the organizational members. They may ask questions like: What is the present situation? What happened in the past? What makes the company successful? What has worked well for the company in the past? These and other exploratory questions communicate to the insider organizational members that the researchers are listening in an open manner and not jumping in with premature interpretations and solutions. An emphasis on exploratory questioning is critical to building the partnership between the parties and demonstrates the practice of engaged scholarship. When there is a sense of a picture being formed and the organizational members feeling comfortable that they are being heard, the researchers may introduce *diagnostic* questioning where they seek not only to draw out the experience of the organizational members but also to understand the members' understanding and interpretations of their experience. Examples of such diagnostic questioning might be: How are you interpreting this event/situation? What does it mean? What is your concern about? How are you judging X to be more important than Y? How does the organization learn from past success? Failures? What are some of the learning processes that are utilized (i.e., post-product development review process; periodic production process, review process, etc.)? A critical process here is for the researchers to pick up how the organizational members are ascribing different meanings to the same experiences and to facilitate the conversations about these differences. Examples of some *confrontational* questions, where the researchers share their perspectives to challenge organizational thinking, might be: You seem to be thinking in terms of problems rather than opportunities, can you explain that? Does that make a difference for you? As we discussed in Chapter 3, such questions are best posed after a relationship has been established through exploratory questioning.

At this stage the researchers are likely not to have built up a sufficient level of trust or knowledge with the insiders to understand the power structure and covert political dynamics among the insiders. Accordingly, spending as much time as possible on exploratory questioning is necessary to avoid making naïve comments that at best demonstrate impressionability and at worst suck them into the organization's internal political agendas. What is also important in this phase of relationship building is that the ground rules for the ethical conduct of the research are articulated. As we introduced in Chapter 3 the researchers need to build psychological safety by assuring the organizational participants of their respect for the anonymity and confidentiality of what they hear, so that, for example, individuals' behaviors unearthed through the inquiry are not used to remove them from the organization. Executive management, in its turn, makes a parallel assurance. At the end of this phase, a basic agreement between the possible project partners is achieved with a further understanding that a study team needs to be created – to include the researchers and members of the organization that can be viewed collectively as a microcosm of the organization – to carry out the next phase of the project.

Phase 2 – Collaborative Exploration of the Context and Its Meaning

Following the initial agreement to go forward with a project, while a basic understanding that the project is likely to shift in its scope and process is agreed upon, a more comprehensive collaborative understanding of the business context takes place. Context here refers to the business, social and academic context of the research. The newly formed study team is likely to focus on developing an understanding of three context areas: the broad general business context at global and national levels; the local organizational/discipline context (i.e., what is going on in the organization); and then the specific topic area. We saw in the vignette in Chapter 1 how capabilities became the focus. The researchers continue in the mode of humble inquiry through exploratory and diagnostic questioning to expose the meanings the organization's insiders ascribe to their experience.

During this phase of the project, developing a shared understanding of the business and social context of the *core* project is very important both in terms of content and process. The researchers guide the process of creating sense-making and shared meaning of the context in which the organization operates by providing a few possible theoretical frameworks (cognitive frames) to choose from, such as sociotechnical systems, resource-based view of systems, contingency perspective, the economic view of the firm, adaptive complex systems perspective, and the like. The data collection and sense-making or meaning creation process needs to be the focus during this phase as it helps in modeling the dialogical practice and can establish the norm of continuous honest conversations. During this phase, the study team articulates the questions that need to asked: What information do you think needs to be collected? What might you expect it to offer to the project? Are there alternative opinions as to what information is required? What might the obstacles be to collecting and interpreting this information? The researchers can then share their expertise in data collection design and interpretation so that agreement can be reached as to what information is to be collected and how.

The study team usually determines how to carry out the data collection and by whom, and, once collected, it deliberates on the data sense-making. In the vignette described in Chapter 1, the study team thought that the external researchers should be the ones to carry out the interviews. In the biopharma case (see Chapter 4), the decision of the study team was that members of the study teams would carry out the interviews, and the external researchers provided basic training in interviewing skills. The researchers are likely to model the dialogical sense-making process and honest conversations. During this phase a collective mindset begins to evolve. By the end of this phase and based on the reflective dialogue and learning, the study team refines a possible focus for what they view as the potential for the most added-value study to the organization.

Phase 3 – Collaborative Re-framing of the Project Purpose, Scope, Research Question/s, Framing of the Inquiry Type, Collaborative Exploration of Research Methodology and the Design of Collaborative Spaces

The outcomes of the learning and new shared understanding and new meaning creation during Phase 2 set the stage for the collaborative thinking and possible re-framing of the project purpose, scope and research question. Having built the partnership through a preponderance of *exploratory* and *diagnostic* questioning, the researchers may draw on *confrontational* questioning appropriately at this phase. Here, the focus is moving towards decision-making and action and the researchers may allow themselves to offer their interpretations and advice as appropriate. Because the relationship has been formed and the practice of engaged scholarship has been built up, offering interpretations or advice is not taken as an expert prescription. Rather, it is taken as an offer of help, which can be assessed on its own merit. At this stage it may be that conversations become dialogues.

As the dialogue and deliberation between the partners are taking place in addressing the above content-related issues, the partners experience and practice what Beer labeled "honest conversations." As such deliberation does not occur in a vacuum, the next challenge is to explore alternative design forums and make choices about appropriate learning mechanisms (what Shani and Docherty (2003) labeled the "learning mechanism tapestry") to be designed and implemented for the ongoing dialogue and deliberations. Since most organizations develop learning mechanisms over time, the leading partners can map up existing learning mechanisms and identify pathways for their utilization as needed. If they choose to supplement the existing learning mechanisms with some others or if they choose to design new learning mechanisms that address the need for cognitive, structural and procedural learning mechanisms, they need to address both how they would aid in addressing the practical issue and facilitate the meaning-making process. All the participants are engaging the general empirical method in consistently questioning each other in order to understand how events are being understood and the reasoning behind the selection of learning mechanisms; that is, testing the abductive reasoning that is being discussed. The external researchers need to be continually testing the level of agreement or consensus in the insider team.

Critical during this phase are also the exploration of options and decisions about the most appropriate inquiry mode, research designs, methodology and timeline. This exploration is also critical in clarifying mutual expectations, desires and goals. This phase concludes with the decision to move forward with the study, agreement on the project study mechanism, sanctioning by the executive team, and its communication to the organization. As we have seen in the vignette in Chapter 1, during this phase the study team generated data documents from the interviews, and based on the interpretations of that data, identified a few central issues. The conversations with the steering committee led to the decision to focus on continuous change and change capabilities. The dialogue led to the recommendation to create two study teams; one that would focus on systematic mapping and assessment of the current change capabilities, while the second would focus on the exploration of possible new change capabilities. The steering committee would lead the study, interfacing with the study teams, executive team and organization members.

Phase 4 – Collaborative Inquiry Process that is Embedded in Data Collection, the Development and Capturing of Systemic Narratives, Generative Images, Meaning Creation, Action Planning and Implementation

Systematic data collection is imperative in the collaborative inquiry process, as the data needs to meet the criteria of validity and reliability. Furthermore, the act of data collection by its very nature stimulates and engages individuals in new ways of thinking and as such can disrupt the ongoing social construction of reality. The learning mechanisms tapestry's critical task during this phase is to design the studies based on their understanding of the company and its culture and adhering to scientific methodological rigor and practice. Beer (2020), for example, suggests that what data to collect, and how and who should collect it, should be part of the combined "task force's" key missions. He further argues that if the intent is to trigger "honest conversations" the task force should not only decide what data to collect, but be the one to actually do so. So, if an *interview methodology* is used as the main data collection source, task force members should be trained in interview methods and be the ones that conduct the interviews.

Similarly, if generative image methodology is used to trigger new experiences for exploration of alternative ways of thinking and acting and new meaning creation, what images should be generated and how they should be generated should be the task of the collaborative study team. Bushe and Marshak (2020) argue that how meaning is made, the language used and the narratives that are created influence the meaning making process, create mindsets and impact behavior. This suggests that a critical part of the collaborative inquiry process is the process of meaning making of the data that is collected as it will impact the essence, direction and system change implementations. In the vignette in Chapter 1, this phase was marked by a shift to generative imagery and the creation of the collages to capture organizational insight. In that story abductive reasoning was expressed through generative imagery. In this phase the researchers are moving in and out of the different inquiry modes as appropriate – sometimes asking exploratory and diagnostic questions and at other times being directly challenging. As always, these are done in the spirit of humble inquiry.

Ongoing reflection on the collaborative inquiry process as it is developing is a critical part of the learning. At times the major issue shifts due to complex business or industry dynamics (MacIntosh et al., 2016). At times it might entail experimentation within alternative collaborative spaces and development of those spaces based on ongoing analysis and sense-making processes (Canterino et al., 2016). Traditional scientific rigor suggests that a clear research design should be crafted and implemented with no or very minimum modifications. As we have advocated earlier, the nature of the emergent process of collaborative inquiry allows for re-framing and re-designing as the project progresses. For example, an initial design might call for inductive or ultimately deductive logic, abductively derived insights, which interrogate the data earlier in the development of knowing, which may be examined carefully within the framework of agreed-upon process to determine what, if any, adjustments to a research design and process are implicated and in what manner might they be implemented without disrupting ongoing processes.

Another illustration is a recent project with a school system that started with a specific research question: What are the characteristics of effective bilingual education? This was changed to: What role does assessment play in the effective delivery of bilingual education? And it finally evolved into: How can teachers involved in bilingual education respond to legislative changes regarding education (MacIntosh et al., 2016)? The research designs and methods changed with the re-framing of each research question by the study teams that led the project. The project lasted three years and led to many changes including change in legislation to the discontinuation of bilingual education in the state, the decision to focus only on one school (not working with multiple schools), a decision to focus on assessment practices and tools, and a change of focus to help teachers prepare for teaching bilingual students in English (MacIntosh et al., 2016).

Phase 5 – Execution of the Changes and Dissemination of the Newly Created Knowledge in Academic and Professional Outlets

The nature of each study is unique, as no two organizations are alike. This suggests extra attention to rigor and documentation of the evolving inquiry story throughout the collaborative inquiry process. We have argued that collaborative inquiry is an engine for organizational or system transformation. The nature and engagement of a wide number of organization members in the inquiry process sets system-wide transformation in motion, as instanced by the school system example.

The execution of the transformation strategy is a process that the executive team leads. The implementation process and its impact need to be studied and improved. As a part of the impact assessment setting in place the continuous learning mechanism to lead such an effort is critical as it provides the organization with the capability to continuously learn and improve. For example, in the vignette in Chapter 1, the executive team adopted the use of study teams to carry out the collaborative assessment of the implementation of the changes, currently in progress.

A further question that needs to be addressed in this phase is the dissemination of the research in publications, of particular interest to the researchers. Three questions are pertinent here. The first is how might the identity of the organization be protected? Secondly, how might the more difficult challenges the organization faced in the project – failures, conflicts, political dynamics – be portrayed? Thirdly, who does the writing? This third question challenges the stereotypes that the researchers do the writing while the participants do the managing. Dissemination is part of the collaborative inquiry contract and so engaging organizational participants in the dissemination processes is highly desirable for the credibility of the research.

The knowledge generated in collaborative inquiry, which, for the most part, follows the Mode 2 paradigm, utilizes abductive logic. The collaborative nature of the process suggests that the dissemination of the newly created and rich insights would add value to theory and inform practice. For example, the project with the school system resulted in the publication of one chapter (MacIntosh et al., 2016) and two articles (MacLean & MacIntosh, 2012; MacLean et al., 2015). Table 5.1 provides a summary of some of the key activities and tools that can be utilized in each phase of the organization development and change process.

QUALITY IN COLLABORATIVE INQUIRY

Collaborative inquiry, as we stated in Chapter 2, is not a new invention, although it continues to be rediscovered by managers, scholars and scholar-practitioners. At the center of collaborative inquiry in organization development practice is dialogue or honest conversation. The challenge (and the opportunity) is to design and manage a dialogical context and process that will be of utmost *relevance* to the partners, be *reflective* in nature and *rigorous*, such that new valid and reliable knowledge – for practice and the scientific community – can be generated. The system's context plays a key role in the establishment of a collaborative inquiry-based effort. Usually not much can be done about it as it reflects the nature and systems within a specific context. Yet, the context for collaboration and dialogue can be designed and managed. For example, alternative collaborative spaces – meaning structures and learning mechanisms – where participants can create collective meaning, and feel safe to explore insights can be investigated, designed and managed. Similarly, as we have argued earlier in this chapter, either individual or collective creation of object/images/artifacts can stimulate individual and collective meaning-making and new insights.

Meaning structures that evolve in systems provide the stage for understanding the essence of dialogue. MacLachlan and Reid (1994) provided three categories of meaning structures: private meaning structures, accessible meaning structures and collective meaning structures. *Private meaning* is the meaning which individuals construct for themselves within a system, which, for a variety of reasons, they decide not to make accessible to others. This might include: meaning that is of a personal nature; meaning that may have been constructed from information that was provided by others; meaning that they may see as providing a competitive advantage; or meaning that they believe will not be relevant

Table 5.1   *Collaborative inquiry: phases, practices and activities*

Phases	Practices and Activities
(0) Preliminary conversation about a possible collaborative project	• Humble conversation about challenges and desires • Sharing mutual expectations (i.e., addressing an organization challenge and researchers need for new knowledge creation and dissemination), roles and timeline • Initial conversation about partnership, collaboration, continuous learning • Initial discussion about the essence of emergent transformation process and broad mapping of a process • Beginning to build trust in the possible partnership
(1) Initial framing and co-framing of project scope around a real system issue/challenge	• Beginning of a mutual education process about the organization's past, present and possible future, and external researchers' world view and knowledge-base • Sharing of opportunities and concerns • Initial sharing of potential added value of building on knowledge-base • Modeling humble inquiry • Initial framing of purpose/research question • Initial exploration of possible learning mechanisms • Initial discussion of the ground rules of a possible collaborative inquiry and ethical conducts are identified and openly discussed • Beginning to build trust in the process • Agreement to proceed
(2) Collaborative exploration of the context (inner and outer) and its meaning	• The creation of a study team comprising insiders and outsiders • Mutual exploration of the business, and social and academic context via exploratory and diagnostic questioning • Developing of shared understanding of the business context and social dynamics, while utilizing a clear theoretical framework (i.e., sociotechnical system, resource-based, economic framework) • Carrying out data collection and data sense-making as modeling the dialogical sense making process, inquiry into ethical conduct, honest conversations and the beginning of the formation of a collaborative mindset • Reflective dialogue based on learning thus far about the most added-value study focus

Phases	Practices and Activities
(3) Collaborative re-framing of the project, framing of the inquiry type, collaborative exploration of research methodology and the design of collaborative spaces	• Collaborative reframing of the project purpose, scope and research question • Exploration and decision about the design of collaborative spaces and/or learning mechanisms tapestry • Exploration and decision about inquiry mode, research designs and methodology • Revisiting mutual expectations about challenges, desires, goals and ethical inquiry practice by all engaged partners • Decision to move forward with the re-defined project scope, process and mechanisms
(4) Collaborative inquiry process that is embedded in data collection, the development and capturing of systematic narratives, generative images, meaning creation, action planning and implementation	• The implementation (creation and establishment) of the collaborative spaces and learning mechanisms tapestry • Training in research methodologies and skills as needed • Collaborative design of data collection tools and processes, as needed • Designing and utilizing generative image or image-based methodology, if used • Systematic data collection process • Systematic collective data sense making process or collective data interpretation process • The development and presentation of recommendations for action and experimentations to the organization executive team
(5) Execution of the changes and dissemination	• Execution of the transformation strategy • Evaluating the implemented changes • Establishing the continuous learning and change process and mechanisms • Discussion about the dissemination of the new knowledge created in publications • Ethical issues to explore about the possible dissemination include: How might the identity of the organization be protected? How will some of the difficult challenges the organization faced in the project be portrayed? Who should be involved in the writing? • Discussing the added value of the dissemination of the newly created knowledge to the wide scholarly-practitioner communities • End of project and termination of the partnership

to others. *Accessible meaning* is the meaning that individuals do make available to other members of the system and, at times, to individuals outside of the system. Norms emerge in the system that allow and sometimes even reinforce the sharing of private meaning. The collaborative inquiry processes of the general empirical method – be attentive to experience, be intelligent in understanding, be reasonable in judging and be responsible in taking action – are enacted through exploratory, diagnostic and confrontational questioning so that private meanings are shared and become accessible to the other partners and move to becoming collective.

Dixon (1999) suggests that "hallways" are places where important private learning is shared. Hallways-based dialogue is an important insight as it brings to the forefront the notion and importance of actual specific physical space for dialogue. *Collective meaning structures* are the meanings created by the collective; they reside in the minds of the system members and the collective as a whole, held in common. Collective meaning ". . . are the norms, strategies and assumptions which specify how work gets done and what work is important to do . . . they may be codified in policies and procedure . . ." (Dixon, 1999: 48).

In Chapters 1 and 4 we briefly discussed the role of learning mechanisms as an arena in which meaning can get created. Learning mechanisms are viewed as formal and informal system arrangements – structures, procedures and processes – that allow systems to systematically collect, analyze, store, disseminate, and use information that is relevant to improve, develop and assimilate learning (Bushe & Shani, 1991; Lipshitz et al., 1996). Learning mechanism tapestries can be designed and implemented to aid the ongoing dialogue and deliberations (Shani & Docherty, 2003). Since most organizations develop learning mechanisms over time, mapping out the existing learning mechanisms and identifying pathways for their utilization is likely to be of added value. At times, the decision is made to supplement the existing learning mechanisms with some others or even to new learning mechanisms to address emergent needs. At their core, learning mechanisms provide a platform, space and capability to carry out and facilitate the meaning-making process. In the vignette in Chapter 1, the learning mechanism that was created was initially composed of a steering committee and a study team. As the project evolved the community decided that they needed to form two study teams instead of one. In the case that was briefly discussed earlier with the telecommunication company (see Chapter 4), the initially created steering committee and study team evolved into a steering committee and three study teams.

Figure 5.2   Quality dimensions of collaborative inquiry

As every form of research has its own criteria of quality, so, too, does collaborative inquiry. How might the quality of a collaborative inquiry be assessed? Figure 5.2 captures the quality dimensions or criteria for collaborative inquiry. Building on Pasmore et al. (2008) and Rajagopalan (2020), we advance a comprehensive framework that can provide an answer. Under *rigorous*, Pasmore et al. (2008) group: data-driven, multiple methodologies, reliability across settings, co-evaluation, causality, underlying mechanisms and publishability. Under *reflective*, they group: historical impact, referential, co-interpretation, community of practice, collection and repeated application. Under *relevant*, they group: practical, co-determined, re-applicable, teachable, face-valid, interesting, true significance and specific. *Resilience*, as advanced by Rajagopalan (2020), is ultimately about persevering and maintaining stability of the process in the face of continuous challenges. Thus, quality of collaborative inquiry can be examined within the context of both the inquiry process and being impactful over time in the face of many challenges placed by managers and scholars alike.

In enacting collaborative inquiry in the present tense and aiming to produce practical knowing that is rigorous, reflective, relevant and resilient, the general empirical method is central (Coghlan, 2010). As we have seen in Chapter 3, this method is grounded in being attentive to data of sense and of consciousness (experience); exploring intelligently to envisage possible explanations of that data (understanding); judging soundly, preferring as probable or certain the explanations that provide the best account for the data (judgment); and being responsible for decisions and actions. When scholar-practitioners and practitioners attend to organizational experiences, converse together to understand, and construct shared meanings, they are enacting the general empirical method. In this manner they are embodying rigor in a science of action and addressing explicitly the pitfalls of working from untested inferences and attributions (Argyris, 2004). Table 5.2 provides a picture of the kinds of questions that may be asked about the central elements of the collaborative inquiry process: the quality of the partnership, the engaged scholarship, inquiring in the present tense, addressing relevant issues and generating practical knowledge and how the elements meet the criteria of rigor, reflective and relevant.

CONCLUSIONS

Following the capturing of collaborative inquiry essence for organization development (Chapter 1), the review of the theoretical underpinning and the philosophical orientation of the social science in organization development, the essence of knowledge creation, Mode 1, Mode 2 and generative change orientations (Chapter 2), the methods of collaborative inquiry (Chapter 3), the transformation and design orientations (Chapter 4), this chapter has focused on the phases, mechanisms and quality of collaborative inquiry. This chapter captures the key phases in the transformation process. We have explored how collaborative inquiry researchers work with members of an organization in the present tense to understand the context and underlying patterns of an organization's experiences as they engage with its members in addressing development

Table 5.2   *Ensuring the quality dimensions of collaborative inquiry*

	Rigorous	Reflective	Relevant	Resilient
Partnership	*What mechanisms are employed to build the relationship between the participants as a genuine partnership? *How are they employed?	How does the collaboration of practitioners and researchers demonstrate the reflective practice of both communities?	How does the focus of the contributing participants remain grounded in the relevant issues?	*How are disagreements within the teams managed? *How are disagreements with other parts of the organization managed? *What mechanisms were designed to sustain continuous learning?
Engaged scholarship/ Humble Inquiry	How are exploratory, diagnostic and confrontational questioning conducted?	How does the inquiry include the interiority of the participants?	How does the collaborative inquiry process remain grounded in the relevant issues?	*Do the researchers maintain the engaged scholarship/ humble inquiry stance and avoid getting sucked into issues of dependency and blaming?
Inquiring in the present tense	How is abductive reasoning engaging with emergent content and process data?	How are the conversations "honest" ones, attending to the "here and now" processes of inquiry and collaboration?	How are the conversations "honest" ones, attending to the critical issues?	*How is the focus on the present maintained and slippage into past thinking avoided? *What processes are developed in order to sustain present tense focus?

	Rigorous	Reflective	Relevant	Resilient
Addressing relevant issues	How are the relevant issues uncovered, assessed and acted upon?	How are the relevant issues reflective of the real issues in the organization's experience?	How are the relevant issues reflective of the real issues confronting the organization?	How is the focus on the relevant issues maintained in the face of political maneuvering?
Generating practical knowledge	How do the rigorous applications of methods and mechanisms ground the quality of the knowledge to be disseminated?	How does the knowledge generated reflect contributions to questions in the literature?	How does the knowledge generated contribute useful knowledge to be field?	*How regularly is the newly generated practical knowledge disseminated throughout the organization?

opportunities or exploring unsolved issues. This chapter has captured the quality dimensions of the change process and has discussed them in the context of each of the six phases and mechanisms of collaborative inquiry for organization development and change practice.

6. The researcher, theorizing and opportunities

Throughout this book we have been exploring the theory and practice of collaborative inquiry for organization development and change. This theory and practice are grounded in conversations and honest dialogue between those who are insiders to the organization and researchers who are outsiders, with the aim of both addressing relevant organizational issues and creating practical knowledge about organizational change. It takes place in the present tense and the role of the researcher is that of an engaged scholar enacting humble inquiry. The general empirical method, described in Chapter 3, operates as the basis for collaborative inquiry. People may inquire into the experiences of others, the insights they have into those experiences and the meanings they attribute to them, the judgments they have made and the consequent actions they have taken. Co-inquiry into what participants have experienced and how they have understood, provides a fruitful approach to developing shared understanding, judgments and planned actions.

Underpinning all this is a philosophy of organizational research that is founded on producing knowledge in the context of application (Coghlan et al., 2020; Shani et al., 2017) and of the researcher as an engaged scholar (Van de Ven, 2007). What does this approach mean for the researcher? How might collaborative researchers think about themselves in this role? How might they be trained or educated to be collaborative researchers? We ground our answer to these questions through the notion of differentiated consciousness, that is, how we know in different ways, a notion we introduced in Chapters 1 and 2 (Coghlan et al., 2019). In this concluding chapter, we focus on the researcher in collaborative inquiry and point to challenges and opportunities for collaborative inquiry as a mechanism for theorizing.

PRACTICAL KNOWING, THEORY AND INTERIORITY

As we explored in Chapter 2, people learn about themselves and the world in diverse ways through different ways of knowing. One way is through the trial and error of everyday living, where they learn experientially (Kolb, 1984). This is the realm of practical knowing and is where most of people's daily engagement occurs. As we discussed in Chapter 2, practical knowing relates to the completion of everyday tasks and their meaning in relation to people's concerns. It seeks to help them deal with situations as they arise and to discover solutions that work. At its core, practical knowing is a descriptive, subject-centered context of knowing; while it is interested in new knowledge creation, it is not interested in universal solutions.

There is also the realm of theory which is the realm of systematic and ordered explanations that are provided by research, what Heron and Reason (1997) called propositional knowing. In the realm of theory, people are interested in things and people not as they relate to them but rather as things relate to one another in a verifiable manner. Explanation has to be accurate, clear and precise so the ambiguities of practical language are averted. Special methods are required to govern different types of investigation and theory generation: deduction from a statistical mode of inquiry to achieve explanation; and an interpretist paradigm whereby understanding, rather than explanation, is sought to establish historical and cultural understanding of specific settings through case-based research.

The critical difference between the two realms is that in the practical mode people are the reference point, e.g., the company is doing well. In the realm of theory the reference point is how things relate to each other, e.g., figures in a balance sheet. Theoretical explanations are incorporated into the books and papers of their respective disciplines and, insofar as they successfully illuminate what is happening, ultimately filter down to become part of the realm of practical know-how.

The realms of practical knowing and of theory provide different and disparate views of the world; for instance, whether the financial figures mean the firm is doing well or not. These realms of meaning are reflected as differentiation of consciousness. In the business and organizational world there is the theoretical world of finance, strategy and effectiveness, which are expressed through performance tests, financial analysis and so on. In the realm of practical knowing there is the experience of learning, success and failure. Both are real and true. The question then is, by what mechanism do people recognize the realm of theory and the realm of practical knowing and be able to move from one realm to another and thereby achieve authentic knowing? The third realm, interiority, emerges as a possible answer to this question.

Interiority is the process whereby people attend to what is going on in themselves as they operate in the realm of practical knowing and the realm of theory. The data they attend to is the cognitional processes within themselves, that is, the data of consciousness. This is a personal process in which they heighten their personal awareness as they undertake the activities of knowing and doing, described in Chapter 3. As we related in that chapter, people can catch themselves in the act of knowing and bring it into their consciousness. Thus, each person can discover that their knowing process operates at four levels: the empirical level of their experiencing, the intelligent level of their understanding, the rational level of their reflection (marshaling evidence and judging) and the responsible level of their decision-making and acting.

The question then arises, how does the notion of differentiation of consciousness and interiority, in particular, inform the work of the researcher in collaborative inquiry? The focus of interiority is to recognize the competence of both practical knowing and theory, and to meet the demands of both without confusing them. Interiority involves shifting from *what* people know to *how* they know, a process of intellectual self-awareness. As instanced in Chapter 1's vignette and examples throughout the book, external researchers can assess financial statements or performance statistics in the realm of theory and notice the insiders' judgments that these figures are not good in the realm of practical knowing. They can appreciate the power of generative imagery. Interiority is characterized by awareness of and reflection on the actual processes of human knowing, and holds each one as valid and true. Included in this attentiveness of how they know are the ethical questions posed in Chapter 3. Holding the questions about maintaining confidentiality and sticking to the values of the partnership involves attention to how they come to make judgments of value, and how these judgments relate to the ways of practical and theoretical ways of knowing.

The distinctive nature of collaborative inquiry involves researchers in differentiated consciousness as they attend to the dynamics of building partnership (the realm of relational knowing), assessing performance standards (theory), exploring the insiders' experiences of the organization (through generative imagery in presentational knowing) and working with them to transform the organization (practical knowing). Creating new collective mindsets through an engagement process triggered by image creation serves as the transformation engine. The notion of interiority as enacted through the general empirical method enables researchers to hold both the science of change and the practice of changing without polarizing them. Research needs to be empirical, theoretical, evaluative, critical and practical. Through understanding these realms of meaning in terms of differentiated consciousness, scholars can stand back from the distinctive foundations and demands of theory (the science of change) and of practical knowing (the practice of changing).

COLLABORATIVE INQUIRY AS A MECHANISM FOR THEORIZING

One of the foundations of collaborative inquiry is that it has a dual purpose; it seeks to be helpful in changing an organizational system and to create practical knowledge through that change process. As we explored in Chapter 2, practical knowing is primary as it integrates other forms of knowing. Through the vignette in Chapter 1 and other examples, we have shown how collaborative inquiry draws on propositional knowing in the scientific data of financial reports and performance metrics. It engages presentational knowing through the creation of generative imagery that engages participants in conversations that give energy and focus to framing a desired future. It is richly enhanced by relational knowing as the insider organizational members and the external researchers build a partnership and engage in dialogue through experience, understanding, judgment, decision and actions. These forms of knowing come together in practical knowing through addressing the challenges facing the organization and articulating learning from the process that is useful for others.

As we discussed in Chapter 2, organization development and change has a dual identity; it is a science of change and an art of changing (Woodman, 2014). As a social science it is eclectic and draws on many forms of scientific investigation and theory formulation: a deductive form of knowledge creation that draws on a statistical mode of inquiry to achieve explanation; an interpretist paradigm for understanding; and action research that understands the purpose of research as generating theory through deliberate engagement in changing. As described in the previous section, interiority enables engaged scholars to appreciate the contribution each form of knowing makes to the collaborative inquiry.

Questions of science can be settled by appealing to observable data. However, in the world of interiority, data are not sensible or observable but belong to the private world of intentional consciousness. Hence, the centrality of exploratory and diagnostic questioning in dialogues in order to bring privately held meanings into a shared space for joint exploration and the creation of collectively shared meaning. Thus, a collaborative engagement in theorizing.

THE SKILLS OF THE RESEARCHER

We are arguing that interiority is a core skill for collaborative researchers. Accordingly, we think it needs to be part of their education and training. As Coghlan et al. (2020) point out, researchers tend to be trained in either Mode 1 or Mode 2 philosophy and methods. To conduct collaborative research researchers need to be able to recognize the scientific nature of some data that is externalized in financial and statistical form, and attend to how they come to a judgment as to the sufficiency and efficacy of that data. They also need to be able to work with the interpretive data of meaning that emerges through reflection on experience and conversations. Knowing the difference is a key skill of interiority.

In Chapter 3, we presented the general empirical method (be *attentive* to experience; be *intelligent* in understanding; be *reasonable* in judging and be *responsible* in taking action). This method is at the heart of interiority as it enables engaged scholars to attend to both data of consciousness (how they are coming to know) and data of sense (what they see and hear). It is through the general empirical method that theory emerges and acts of theorizing occur.

Theory

Collaborative inquiry contains an explicit focus on theory that is generated from the conceptualization of the particular experience in ways that are intended to be meaningful to others. In collaborative inquiry the emergent theory is situation specific. It emerges naturally through the implementation and outcomes of the partnership engaging in inquiry and actions as they occur in the present tense. It emerges through abductive reasoning in the face of surprises with the messiness and anomalies of the developing situation in the collaborative and change process, and how the participants process their questions and engage with one another and articulate how they come to know.

Theorizing

Swedberg (2014) makes the case that the act of theorizing is generally neglected with the emphasis being generally placed on the theory as the outcome, rather than the process of getting there. He argues for attention to be given to the process of theorizing, i.e., the process of what one does when producing a theory, an argument supported by Hansen and Madsen (2019). The act of theorizing or model creation turns the attention from the outcome to the act of generation itself. It places the issue firmly in the question, "How do we come to know?"; in other words, interiority. As Coghlan et al. (2019) demonstrate, each act of knowledge of concrete reality includes questioning, understanding, critically reflecting and concluding. By attending to both the data of their consciousness (how they are experiencing, questioning, understanding and judging) as well as to the data of sense (what they see and hear in the external data) committed scholars can engage with the empirical data of their experiencing, the intellectual data of their understanding (by abductive reasoning in the context of discovery) and the rational data of their judgments (by inductive reasoning in the context of verification).

CHALLENGES AND OPPORTUNITIES

Collaborative inquiry as presented in this book does not reflect an easy process of organization development and change. Yet, its comprehensive all-engaged orientation, which is embedded in the present tense and the development of new mindsets by means of the collaborative inquiry and discovery process, serves as a powerful engine of transformation and plays a critical role in advancing theory and practice. The current state of our knowledge suggests the need to conduct research that pushes the boundaries of our vision, so that all involved are stimulated to further explore the possibilities and opportunities that collaborative inquiry presents.

The Epistemological and Methodological Challenge

Different forms of reasoning have been identified in the literature, such as inductive, deductive, pragmatic, instrumental, transcendental, reflective and abductive (Coghlan et al., 2019; Shani et al., 2020). In Chapters 2 and 3 we argued that abductive reasoning plays a critical role in Mode 2 organization development and change research orientation. We view organizations as complex adaptive sociotechnical systems composed of interacting humans, using knowledge, technology and tools to produce goods or services valued by customers. In Chapter 1, we further argued that organizations are social constructions, artifacts created by human beings to serve their ends. As such, they are, in effect, communities created by meaning, with a rich tapestry of cultural rules, roles and interactions (Schein & Schein, 2017).

Collaborative researchers in association with members of the organization act as the co-designers and co-facilitators of the project. Such an orientation, although it fits well within Mode 2 research orientation, is likely to be problematic for those that hold a Mode 1 orientation and who seek "objective truth." Careful examination of collaborative inquiry practices, as demonstrated in Chapter 5, illustrate that methodological rigor is held throughout the inquiry process. Unlike Mode 1 researchers, we advocate that it is possible to do research *with* rather than *on* an organization. Such research practices, in addition to generating useful knowledge, serve as an engine for organization transformation. Design, implementation and documentation of such effort by the organization development and change community are likely to enhance the impact and legitimacy of the field.

The Emergent and Interlevel Perspectives

As we have seen in this book, partnership formations and their quality are critical in the collaborative inquiry process. In some ways, the formation of new partnership occurs at many levels, between researchers and members of the organization, between the executive team members, between the management team and organizational members, and between members of the organization from different units and hierarchical levels. Partnerships tends to develop over time, and so their quality and outcomes. The collaborative nature of the effort's joint discovery process across all levels sets the context and space where working through conflicts that are routed in legitimate differences enhances the quality of the relationship and the quality of the new insights generated.

New understanding develops over time and, as such, it is not uncommon that the nature and direction of the project changes (MacIntosh et al., 2016). This emergent quality of the project fits well within the natural evolution of any social system. As we have seen throughout this book, the emergent quality of a collaborative inquiry orientation is one of the key features that differentiates it from traditional research orientations. While it is critical to initiate the project with a clear intent/focus/research question, it is just as critical to be open to shift focus as the project evolves, hence the value of abductive reasoning. Documenting the process by means of comprehensive diaries by the partners can become an important database upon which one can create and disseminate the new knowledge to be generated to the larger scholarly community.

Methodologies, Methods and Generative Images

As we pointed out in Chapter 3, a method provides a key to the relationship between questioning and answering (Coghlan, 2010). We have presented the general empirical method as a framework for engaging with the differentiated ways of knowing that are at the heart of collaborative inquiry. Through their interiority, collaborative researchers can hold the different ways of knowing that occur in a project: the scientific data of financial and performance, the presentational data of generative images and envisioning, the relational data of how the partnership is developing, and the quality of the honest conversations and the practical data of what is working. Each of these ways of knowing answers different questions. How valid and reliable is financial and performance data? How do we understand and hold together the different meanings attributed to organizational events? How do we build trust and collaboration between the insiders and external researchers? How do we appreciate generative images? What will we do?

As was suggested in Chapters 2 and 3, generative images can play an important role in the collaborative inquiry process. Creating the space for the creation of images – whether they are pictures, collages, multi-layer carpets, stories, sculptures – tends to trigger the development of new insights and cognitive mindsets. Thus, incorporating the creative process of image creation as part of the methodological rigor generates opportunity for reflection and enhances the relevancy-based dialogue (Adler & Delbecq, 2017). The benefit of the general empirical method is that it situates inquiry as what we recognize as the normal activities of human knowing, and it encompasses the ways of knowing that we employ in different settings.

CONCLUSIONS

We have presented collaborative inquiry as a philosophy, a social science and a series of methods in and for the field of organization development and change. Although it has been practiced in various forms and with different variations over the last seven decades, its potential has not been fully realized and it has not found its way into mainstream researcher education. Few organizations or scholars, to our knowledge, have fully embraced the concept, or its philosophical, social science foundation and its potential impact. Yet, as the preceding chapters have shown, many scholars and organization development and change projects around the globe have incorporated some elements of them in different shapes and forms.

We have attempted to lay out a broad framework with its foundational tenets based on our collective 60 years of reflected experience as scholar-practitioners. Our hope is that we have captured the opportunity and benefits for all those who may want to enhance their ability to make a difference for practice and for theory in the emerging complex future of organizations, communities and society at large.

Epilogue

Throughout this book we have been mapping the theory and practice of collaborative inquiry. As we been exploring, a significant discovery during a collaborative inquiry process occurs when the organizational members generate pictorial expressions in the form of images. These images, the expression of presentational knowing, articulate the organization and its desired future in creative visual terms and enable the organizational members to have rich shared insight into the potential of the project. As we have been reviewing and revising draft chapters in the process of bringing our collaborative venture to completion and submitting it to the publishers, an image of an olive tree emerged for us. This generative image excited us as we explored it and attempted to draw it.

COLLABORATIVE INQUIRY AS AN OLIVE TREE

The tree itself expresses the process of collaborative inquiry as summarized in Chapter 1. The roots of the tree are the theoretical foundations captured in Chapter 2: organizations as social learning systems and Mode 2 knowledge production of organization development and change within a social science philosophy. The lower part of the trunk, as captured in Chapter 4 expresses the essence of transformation, transformation process and design orientations. The middle section of the trunk, captured in Chapter 3 and sections of Chapters 2 and 4, expresses the methodology and methods through humble inquiry, the general empirical method, and many ways of knowing, particularly practical knowing and inquiring in the present tense. The upper trunk, captured in Chapter 5, expresses the enactment of design through the six phases in the transformation process. The protruding branches with their leaves and fruit capture the focus on the outcomes of helping the organization address a concrete challenge and achieve transformational change, develop new capabilities, thereby generating new practical knowledge.

Source: Artwork by Jayne Behman, 2020.

Figure E.1   Collaborative inquiry as an olive tree

The olive tree symbolizes the essence as well as the source of life in many regions, religions and cultures. Some argue that the olive tree is one of the oldest symbols in the world with a wide range of meaning such as strength, wisdom, health, timelessness, success, longevity, nutrition, everlasting green leaves, a never ending olive producer, a source of shade, and more. An evergreen and golden dark green *olive leaf* has endured as the *symbol of peace and prosperity. When observing olive trees, one also realizes that there are no two olive trees alike.* In Greek mythology, the evergreen and golden dark green *olive leaf* also endured as the *symbol of peace, prosperity and balance.* Arriving at this concluding part of the book, you as reader are invited to add your interpretation to the olive tree and/or create your own metaphor that captures your learning and insights about the essence of collaborative inquiry. For us, the dynamic nature of collaborative inquiry for organization development and change initiative can be thought of as an olive tree that offers the environment theory and everlasting practice of organizational transformation and of continuous practical knowledge production.

Afterword: Collaborative inquiry: takeaways and applications

Philip H. Mirvis[1]

Organization Development (OD) was born from a creative amalgam of ideas and practices from systems theory, group dynamics, counseling psychology, and a scientific/medical model of diagnosis and problem solving. In this volume, Shani and Coghlan have reimagined the field with an inventive synthesis of new theory and perspectives and their own unique scholarship and insights. As you've read, they present collaborative inquiry in a clear flow from its foundations to methods to applications. But this neat packaging is deceptively simple. In truth, it has taken hard and original thinking aided by user-friendly modeling to pull this all together. I am both envious of and grateful to them for their contribution to theory and practice.

In reflecting on their own collaborative inquiry, I address four personal takeaways: (1) what we already know but now see in new ways; (2) what we did not know but now do; (3) how we might apply this knowledge; and (4) what it takes to produce a summative statement.

1.   WHAT WE ALREADY KNOW BUT NOW SEE IN NEW WAYS

We know that creative thinking relies on different mental models and tools than critical thinking (Csikzentmihalyi, 1996; Ruggiero, 1999) and have been advised to take different approaches to solving complex (aka ill-defined, wicked, adaptive) problems versus routine (aka structured, unambiguous, technical) ones (Rittel & Webber, 1973; Heifetz & Heifetz, 1994; Conklin, 2006). But how about inquiries into situations that feature both kinds of problems and call for multiple ways of thinking and knowing?

The authors' collaborative inquiry with Mia and her agricultural machinery company provides some lessons in these instances. Searching for better "change capabilities," two sub-teams in the company respectively examined (1) past practices in managing change and (2) new capabilities that might be developed. The group looking at past practices conducted an "autopsy" on prior change events by interviewing key participants, compiling findings across the events, and then administering a survey covering some 25 change capabilities that respondents ranked from most to least critical. Inquiry: Logical, rational, scientific.

By contrast, team members exploring new change capabilities brought artifacts and images of new practices into a session where, with the assistance of a graphic artist, they merged them into three collages that reflected the essence of desired practices. The team then enlisted others around the organization in a session where each was asked to write a story about how a new practice might be used, read it aloud, and then engaged in "collective sense-making" with other participants. Inquiry: Creative, emotive, aesthetic.

Here we see two different problems met with two different types of inquiry and might draw from this a contingency theory for when to pitch thinking toward creativity and when not. But, look at the case again, and you see that the group engaged in routine inquiry also sketched their analyses – in the form of a flow chart, a quilt, a craft maneuvering through white water, a group hiking up a mountain, and so forth. Why so? As the author's note, "people are quite engaged when they make things – words, stories, pictures, artifacts." Meanwhile, the group that created a collage and told stories followed this up with a logical list of generated change capabilities and joined with the other group to identify what skills, practices, and processes might be required to exercise them.

By this example, Shani and Coghlan nudge us to think of collaborative inquiry as a "whole brain" activity. Certainly a mix of left- and right-brain activities in whatever kind of problem is investigated gives ample opportunity for people who are either more verbal or more visual to share their gifts and feel included in the process. Bruner (2009) distinguishes between two different modes of thought: Logico-scientific and Narrative. The former is theory-driven and engages the world with if–then, cause–effect logic. It operates with reason, sound argument, and tight analysis. The latter is meaning-centered and interprets the world experientially and vicariously. It operates with intuition, metaphors and practical knowledge. Which one is better suited to collaborative inquiry? Both.

Sequencing is a consideration. Aristotle tells us, "The soul . . . never thinks without a picture." Presentational forms of expression such as storytelling, drawing, music, and drama are ideally suited to tapping into and representing people's tacit knowledge of themselves, other people, and the world around them. Propositional knowledge, in turn, makes this more explicit in the form of facts, findings, abductions, and theories about problems and possible solutions. Taken together, these two kinds of knowledge give inquirers a fuller understanding of the situation at hand (Gagliardi, 1996; Taylor & Hansen, 2005).

This whole brain strategy and sequencing seems to be deployed by the authors who first present us with Mia's case study to ground our intuitions and later detail the mixing of evidence and insights, verbal and nonverbal knowing, and questions and answers in showing us how to negotiate meaning in collaborative inquiry. Then they take us into design thinking and illustrate this interplay in creating something new.

A second thing we already know is that individual and collective predilections and biases inform and can hamper collaborative inquiry. These can take the form of an implicit bias like stereotyping or natural tendencies to search for, focus on and remember information in a way that confirms one's preconceptions (Nickerson, 1998; Greenwald et al., 2002). Manifestations in collectives include groupthink and defensive reasoning (Janis, 1972; Argyris, 1985). Accordingly, those who guide collaborative inquiries alert individuals to be aware of their thoughts and emotions as they inquire and to self-scan. Many also carve out time and space, including "time-outs," in which a group can reflect on its operations and doings.

A first reading of this counsel is that its aim is to "correct" biases that can impede a true reading of the situation and short-circuit collective dynamics that might prevent open, honest, and unconstrained analyses and discussion. Yes, but . . . there is an affirmative side to this as well. With the introduction of the concept of interiority, Shani and Coghlan urge inquirers to attend to their thinking and engagement with the questions posed not just to eliminate bias but also to better access their imagination, intuitions, and nonconscious ways of seeing and knowing themselves and the world.

These can be a source of generative thinking and insight for inquiry and it also enables inquirers to envision a better world and enact their better selves. The authors tell us:

> Meaning can be viewed as the internal cognitive and emotional structures of ideas and feelings that allow a person to understand a version of the world, as

manifest as a representation of the way things are and the way they ought to be and that places the person into this world version.

On this count, Karl Weick (1996) advises inquirers to "drop your tools" of linear thinking and rationality when confronted with a problem. And one of my mentors, M. Scott Peck (1987), advises people to "empty" themselves of preconceptions, expectations, and answers as they inquire into themselves as a community. Both of these methods allow something new and unforeseen to enter an inquiring space.

Note to those who facilitate collaborative inquiry: In Mia's organization, inquirers were given some cognitive inputs about "change capability" to inform their investigations and recommendations. It also helps to give participants some inputs on metacognition – how to think about their thinking and be fully present in this work. Collectively establishing "rules of engagement" for inquiry and dialogue can be helpful.

2.   WHAT WE DID NOT KNOW BUT NOW DO

We know that there are different ways of knowing but we don't know how these ought to be applied in collaborative inquiry. The authors tell us that accomplishing different tasks relies on distinct ways of knowing:

- building partnership (relational knowing);
- assessing performance standards (theoretical knowing);
- exploring insiders' experiences of their organization (presentational knowing); and
- working with them to transform the organization (practical knowing).

In the same vein, they make a case for sequencing dialogue in collaborative inquiry through exploratory to diagnostic to confrontational phases and present us with orienting questions keyed to each phase. In so doing, they provide us what Mike Beer (1992) calls both useful *and* usable knowledge for practice.

But putting this knowledge into practice isn't easy. Early in the volume Shani and Coghlan remind us of the concept of *ba*, popularized by Nonaka and Konno (1998), which represents a "space" (physical, mental, relational, virtual) in which knowledge can be shared, created and used. They argue, too, that conditions of "psychological safety" enable people to present more of their ideas and themselves into this space. But the idea has been appropriated into education and conversation where "trigger warnings" must be issued before raising controversial subjects and speakers are expected to be "politically correct" in what they say and how they express themselves. Does an emphasis on psychological safety mean that all our inquiries must be conducted squarely in the "comfort zone"?

Instead, I would argue that psychological safety provides an emotional foundation for the open expression of diverse ideas, challenging questions, and topics that generate conversational friction – all essential to collective learning (Mirvis, 2002). A group committed to reflective inquiry can serve as a "container" that holds differences and conflicts up for ongoing exploration. This keeps "hot" conversation "cooled" sufficiently that people can see the "whole" of what is on the group mind. By simultaneously self-scanning and inquiring with a group, its members create a cohesive connective field among themselves and more fully investigate what their inquiry is producing.

Another thing we now know? Hats off to Bob Marshak and Gervase Bushe for so thoughtfully theorizing dialogic OD. But what has been missing is how to deploy dialogic OD in collaborative inquiry where the aim is not just to talk together better but to solve a real-time problem. Now we know what to do as the authors present a six-phase process and give us the gear and guidelines needed to conduct a collaborative inquiry. Pay attention to their emphasis on creating a governing structure – including executive sponsorship, a steering committee, a work timetable, and defined deliverables – to support a collaborative inquiry and ensure that its findings translate into action. A long-favored way to avoid solving a problem is to commission a group to "study" it and then subsequently "file" the results.

3.   HOW WE MIGHT APPLY THIS KNOWLEDGE

In this volume, Shani and Coghlan illustrate collaborative inquiry primarily in OD projects within a business. In other reports, they shows its use in an Italian social cooperative, health care and hospitals, a merger of two organizations, in social inquiry groups on campuses and in communities, and as a component of diverse action research projects. I wish I had access to their criteria of "quality" in collaborative inquiry when appraising and comparing a diverse series of collaborative sustainability projects published in a book on *Building Networks and Partnerships* (Worley & Mirvis, 2013). Their concepts, models and methods are generalizable to diverse efforts where people come together to think and collaboratively solve problems.

Beyond applications to organization change and improvement, three other arenas of application are hinted at but invite further consideration and research. For instance, T-groups have gone out of fashion in OD but dialogue and collaborative inquiry are integral to the workings of self-help groups, forums on diversity and inclusion, community building activities, truth-and-reconciliation efforts, and peacemaking. Ed Schein (2009b, 2013) has expanded his thinking on process consultation to apply to helping more broadly and humble inquiry. If not the authors, then perhaps you the reader might take the ideas advanced here and consider how they apply to understanding and assisting those who engage in collaborative inquiry for the sake of self-knowing, healing, bridging differences, spiritual growth, or social progress.

A second arena for application concerns virtual inquiries, where participants dialogue online in real time or asynchronously on myriad topics ranging from work-related problems to interpersonal mores to what is happening with the spread of Covid-19. Here the articulation of rules of engagement is essential and may require monitoring in cases of gaslighting, culture jamming and trolling. Who is responsible for process facilitation and how do you move a virtual conversation from monologues to debates to dialogue? Let's take these ideas on collaborative inquiry and see their applications and limits in online communities.

Finally, there are applications in collaborative research between scholars and practitioners to consider. Shani and Coghlan have given us droplets throughout on how OD researchers can engage with practitioners in collaborative inquiry in action research. They have written much more on this in other outlets and volumes, so if this is an interest of yours please peruse their bibliography.

But recognize if you are a doctoral student, early-career professor, or scholar-practitioner working in an organization but angling toward academe, that research based on collaborative inquiry with practitioners is *not* a traditional ticket to "A" journal publication and academic advancement. But the authors were not deterred by this and neither were Garima Sharma and Pratima (Tima) Bansal (2020) who leapt across the academic–practice gap in a 2018 study of, interestingly, how researchers and practitioners think, talk and work together – and earned kudos for it.

4.   WHAT IT TAKES TO PRODUCE A SUMMATIVE STATEMENT (AND WHY IT IS NOT EASY TO DO)

To the extent that research is depicted as a science and practice as an art, Shani and Coghlan blend these orientations into a third archetype: scholarship as craft. You've seen how these two combine a deep knowledge of social science and its methods with an experiential understanding of action and organizational doings to produce scholarship that is interesting, thought provoking, and (to my eyes) remarkably true to life.

It is speculative, but I see these two as an "odd couple" whose different interests and ways of looking at the world have contributed to their synthesizing ideas. Scholarly collaborations have different trajectories. Mine, with Mitchell Marks, started with a bang when we pioneered the study of the human side of mergers, but while our continuing collaboration provided some fresh case material, it added only footnotes to our original theorizing (Mirvis & Marks, 2017). Shani and Coghlan, by comparison, began their studies of collaborative inquiry modestly and matter-of-factly and then added novelty and nuance to their thinking and verisimilitude to their field research. This summative volume is full of fireworks – bursting with authority and color and attesting to the creative potential of a true, sustained co-mingling of minds.

NOTE

1. Fellow at Global Network on Corporate Citizenship; Babson Social Innovation Lab.

References

Ackerman, A.L. & Anderson, D. (2001). *The change leader's roadmap: How to navigate your organization's transformation.* San Francisco, CA: Wiley.

Adler, N.J. & Delbecq, A.L. (2017). Twenty-first century leadership: A return to beauty. *Journal of Management Inquiry,* 27(2), 119–37.

Antal, A., Dierkes, M., Child, J. & Nonaka, I. (2001). Introduction. In A. Antal, M. Dierkes, J. Child & I. Nonaka (Eds.), *Handbook of organizational learning and knowledge* (pp. 1–10). New York: Oxford University Press.

Argyris, C. (1985). *Strategy, change and defensive routines.* Boston: Pitman Publishing.

Argyris, C. (2004). *Reasoning and rationalizations.* New York: Oxford University Press.

Argyris, C. (2010). *Organizational traps.* New York: Oxford University Press.

Argyris, C. & Schon, D.A. (1996). *Organizational learning II.* Reading, MA: Addison-Wesley.

Bailey, K.D. (1978). *Methods of social research.* New York: The Free Press.

Bartunek, J.M. (1984). Changing interpretive schemes and organizational restructuring: The example of a religious order. *Administrative Science Quarterly,* 29, 355–72.

Bartunek, J.M. & Jones, E.B. (2017). How organizational transformation has been continuously changing and not changing. In A.B. (Rami) Shani & D.A. Noumair (Eds.), *Research in organizational change and development* (Vol. 25, pp. 143–69). Bingley, UK: Emerald.

Bartunek, J.M. & Louis, M.R. (1988). The interplay of organizational development and organizational transformation. In W.A. Pasmore & R.W. Woodman (Eds.), *Research in organizational change and development* (Vol. 2, pp. 97–137). Greenwich, CT: JAI Press.

Bartunek, J.M. & Rynes, S.L. (2014). Academics and practitioners are alike and unlike: The paradoxes of academic-practitioner relationships. *Journal of Management,* 40, 1181–201.

Beckhard, R. (1969). *Organization development: Strategies and models.* Reading, MA: Addison-Wesley.

Beer, M. (1980). *Organization change and development: A systems view.* Santa Monica, CA: Goodyear.

Beer, M. (1992). Strategic-change research: An urgent need for usable rather than useful knowledge. *Journal of Management Inquiry,* 1(2), 111–16.

Beer, M. (2014). OD at a crossroads. *OD Practitioner,* 46(4), 60–61.

Beer, M. (2020). *Fit to compete: Why honest conversations about your company's capabilities are the key to a winning strategy.* Boston, MA: Harvard Business Review Press.

Beer, M., Eisenstat, R. & Spector, B. (1990). *The critical path to corporate renewal*. Boston, MA: Harvard Business School Press.

Bennis, W.G. (1969). *Organization development: Its nature, origins and prospects*. Reading, MA: Addison-Wesley.

Bertalanffy, L. (1950). The theory of open systems in physics and biology. *Science*, 111, 23–9.

Bohm, D. (1989). *On dialogue*. Ojai, CA: Ojai Institute Publication.

Bradbury, H. (2015). *The Sage handbook of action research*. 3rd edn. London: Sage.

Bradbury, H. & Mainmelis, C. (2001). Learning history and organizational praxis. *Journal of Management Inquiry*, 10, 340–57.

Bradbury, H., Mirvis, P., Neilsen, E. & Pasmore, W. (2008). Action research at work: Creating the future following the path from Lewin. In P. Reason & H. Bradbury (Eds.), *The Sage handbook of action research*, 2nd edn. (pp. 77–92). London: Sage.

Brown, J. (1995). Dialogue: Capacities and stories. In S. Chawla & J. Benesch (Eds.), *Learning organizations: Developing cultures for tomorrow's workplace* (pp. 153–64). Portland, OR: Productivity Press.

Bruner, J.S. (2009). *Actual minds, possible worlds*. Cambridge, MA: Harvard University Press.

Bruning, R.H. (1994). The college classroom from the perspective of cognitive psychology. In K.W. Prichard & R.M. Sawyer (Eds.), *The handbook of college teaching: Theory and applications* (pp. 3–22). London: Greenwood Press.

Buono, A.F. & Kerber, K.W. (2008). The challenges of organizational change: Enhancing organizational change capacity, *Revue Science de Gestion*, 65, 99–118.

Burnes, B. & Cooke, B. (2012). The past, present and future of organization development: Taking the long view. *Human Relations*, 65, 1395–429.

Burns, T. & Stalker, G.M. (1961). *The management of innovation*. London: Tavistock.

Bushe, G.R. (2013). Dialogic OD: A theory of practice. *OD Practitioner*, 45(1), 11–17.

Bushe, G.R. & Marshak, R.J. (2009). Revisioning organization development: Diagnostic and dialogic premises and patterns of practice. *Journal of Applied Behavioral Science*, 45, 348–68.

Bushe, G.R. & Marshak, R.J. (2014). The dialogic mindset in organization development. In A.B. (Rami) Shani and D.A. Noumair (Eds.), *Research in organizational change and development* (Vol. 22, pp. 55–97). Bingley, UK: Emerald.

Bushe, G.R. & Marshak, R.J. (2015). *Dialogic organization development: The theory and practice of transformational change*. Oakland, CA: Berrett-Koehler.

Bushe, G.R. & Marshak, R.J. (2020). *Dialogic organization development: Companion booklet to the BMI Series in Dialogic OD*. North Vancouver, BC: Bushe–Marshak Institute.

Bushe, G. & Shani, A.B. (Rami) (1991). *Parallel learning structures: Creating innovations in bureaucracies*. Reading, MA: Addison-Wesley.

Cameron, K.S. & Quinn, R.E. (2011). *Diagnosing and changing organizational culture: Competing values framework*. San Francisco, CA: Jossey Bass.

Campbell, D. (2000). *The socially constructed organization.* London: Karnac.

Canterino, F., Shani, A.B. (Rami), Coghlan, D. & Brunelli, M. (2016). Collaborative management research as a modality of action research: Learning from a merger-based study. *Journal of Applied Behavioral Science*, 52(2), 157–86.

Checkland, P. (1981). *System thinking, system practice.* New York: Wiley.

Cirella, S., Canterino, F., Guerci, M. & Shani, A.B. (Rami) (2016). Organizational learning mechanisms and creative climate: Insights from an Italian fashion design company. *Creativity and Innovation Management*, 25(2), 221–2.

Cirella, S., Guerci, M. & Shani, A.B. (Rami) (2012). A process model of collaborative management research: The study of collective creativity in the luxury industry. *Systematic Practice and Action Research*, 25(1), 281–300.

Coghlan, D. (2009). Toward a philosophy of clinical inquiry/research. *Journal of Applied Behavioral Science*, 45(1): 106–21.

Coghlan, D. (2010). Seeking common ground in the diversity and diffusion of action and collaborative management research methodologies: The value of a general empirical method. In W.A. Pasmore, A.B. (Rami) Shani & R.W. Woodman (Eds.), *Research in organization change and development* (Vol. 18, pp. 149–81). Bingley, UK: Emerald.

Coghlan, D. (2012). Organization development and action research: Then and now. In D. Boje, B. Burnes & J. Hassard (Eds.), *The Routledge companion to organizational change* (pp. 47–58). Abingdon: Routledge.

Coghlan, D. (2016). Retrieving the philosophy of practical knowing for action research. *International Journal of Action Research*, 12(1), 84–107.

Coghlan, D. (2017). Insight and reflection as key to collaborative engagement. In J.M. Bartunek and J. McKenzie (Eds.), *Academic practitioner research partnerships: Developments, complexities and opportunities* (pp. 36–49). Abingdon: Routledge.

Coghlan, D. (2019). *Doing action research in your own organization.* 5th edn. London: Sage.

Coghlan, D. & Shani, A.B. (Rami) (2017). Inquiring in the present tense: The dynamic mechanism of action research. *Journal of Change Management*, 17(2), 121–37.

Coghlan, D. & Shani, A.B. (Rami) (2018). *Conducting action research.* London: Sage.

Coghlan, D., Shani, A.B. (Rami) & Dahm, P.C. (2020). Knowledge production in organization development: An interiority-based perspective. *Journal of Change Management*, 20(1), 81–98.

Coghlan, D., Shani, A.B. (Rami) & Hay, G.W. (2019). Toward a social science philosophy of organization development and change. In D.A. Noumair & A.B. (Rami) Shani (Eds.), *Research in organizational change and development* (Vol. 27, pp. 1–29). Bingley, UK: Emerald.

Cohen, M.D. & Sproull, L.S. (Eds.) (1996). *Organizational learning.* London: Sage.

Collatto, D., Dresch, A., Lacerda, D. & Bentz, I. (2017). Is action design research indeed necessary? Analysis and synergies between action research and design science research. *Systemic Practice and Action Research*, 31(3), 239–67.

Conklin, J. (2006). *Dialogue mapping: Building shared understanding of wicked problems*. Chichester, UK: John Wiley & Sons.

Cooperrider, D. (2017). The gift of new eyes: Personal reflections after 30 years of appreciative inquiry in organizational life. In A.B. (Rami) Shani & D. Noumair (Eds.), *Research in organizational change and development* (Vol. 25. pp. 81–142). Bingley, UK: Emerald.

Coughlan, P. & Coghlan, D. (2011). *Collaborative improvement through network action learning*. Cheltenham, UK and Northampton, MA, USA: Edward Elgar Publishing.

Cronin, B. (2017). *Phenomenology of human understanding*. Eugene, OR: Pickwick.

Cross, R., Taylor, S. & Zehner, D. (2018). Collaboration without burnout. *Harvard Business Review*, 96(4), 134–7.

Csikzentmihalyi, M. (1996). *Creativity: Flow and the psychology of discovery and invention*. New York: HarperCollins.

Cummings, T.G. (Ed.) (2008). *Handbook of organization development*. Thousand Oaks, CA: Sage.

de Geus, A. (1998). *The living company*. Boston, MA: Harvard Business Press.

Dixon, N.M. (1999). *The organizational learning cycle: How we can learn collectively*. Brookfield, VT: Gower.

Docherty, P. & Shani, A.B. (Rami) (2008). Learning by design: A fundamental foundation for organization development change programs. In T.G. Cumming (Ed.), *Handbook of organization development* (pp. 163–81). Thousand Oaks, CA: Sage.

Drath, W.H. & Palus, C.J. (1994). *Making common sense: Leadership as meaning-making in a community of practice*. Greensborough, NC: Center for Creative Leadership Press.

Dresch, A., Lacerda, D. & Antunes, Jr, J. (2014). *Design science research: A method for science and technology advancement*. Cham: Springer International Publishing.

Drew, S. & Guillemin, M. (2014). From photographs to findings: Visual meaning-making and interpretive engagement in the analysis of participant-generated images. *Visual Studies*, 29(1), 54–67.

Emery, F. & Trist, E. (1965). The causal textures of organizational environments. *Human Relations*, 18, 21–31.

Fredberg, T., Norrgren, F. & Shani, A. B. (Rami) (2011). Developing and sustaining change capability via learning mechanisms: A longitudinal perspective on transformation. In R.W. Woodman, W.A. Pasmore & A.B (Rami) Shani (Eds.), *Research in organizational change and development* (Vol. 19, pp. 117–61). Bingley, UK: Emerald.

Freeman, R.E., Wicks, A.C., Harrison, J., Parmar, B. & DeColle, S. (2010). *Stakeholder theory: The state of the art*. New York: Cambridge University Press.

French, W.L. & Bell, C.H. (1990). *Organization development: Behavioral science interventions for organization improvement*. 4th edn. Englewood Cliffs, NJ: Prentice-Hall.

Friedlander, F. & Brown, L.D. (1974). Organization development. *Annual Review of Psychology*, 25, 313–41.

Friedman, V., Lipshitz, R. & Overmeer, W. (2001). Creating conditions for organizational learning. In A. Antal, M. Dierkes, J. Child & I. Nonaka (Eds.), *Handbook of organizational learning and knowledge* (pp. 757–74). New York: Oxford University Press.

Friedman, V.J., Sykes, I., Lapidot-Lefler, N. & Haj, N. (2016). Social space as a generative image for dialogic organization development. In D.A. Noumair & A.B. (Rami) Shani (Eds.), *Research in organizational change and development* (Vol. 24, pp. 113–44). Bingley, UK: Emerald.

Gagliardi, P. (1996). Exploring the aesthetic side of organizational life. In S.R. Clegg, C. Hardy & W.R. Nord (Eds.), *Handbook of organization studies* (pp. 701–24). London: Sage.

Galbraith, J.R. (1995). *Designing organizations.* San Francisco, CA: Jossey-Bass.

Galuppo, L., Gorli, M., Alexander, B. & Scaratti, G. (2019). Leading in social entrepreneurship: Developing organizational resources in confrontation with paradoxes. In A.B (Rami) Shani & D.A. Noumair (Eds.), *Research in organizational change and development* (Vol. 27, pp. 167–86). Bingley, UK: Emerald.

Gavin, D.A. (2000). *Learning in action: A guide to putting the learning organization to work.* Boston, MA: Harvard Business Review Press.

Gergen, K.J. (1978). Toward generative theory. *Journal of Personality and Social Psychology*, 36(11), 1344–60.

Gibbons, M., Limoges, C., Nowotny, H., Schartzman, S., Scott, P. & Trow, M. (1994). *The new production of knowledge.* London: Sage.

Gibbons, M., Limoges, C. & Scott, P. (2011). Revisiting mode 2 at Noors Slott. *Prometheus*, 29(4), 361–72.

Goodman, N. (1976). *Ways of worldmaking.* Indianapolis, IN: Hackett Publishing.

Grant, R.M. (1996). Prospering in dynamically competitive environments: Organizational capability as knowledge integrators. *Organization Science*, 7, 375–87.

Gray, B. (1989). *Collaborating: Finding common ground for multiparty problems.* San Francisco, CA: Jossey-Bass.

Greenbaum, B., Shani, A.B. (Rami) & Verganti, R. (2020). Radical circles: Engines for organizational transformation? *Organization Development Review*, 52(3), 53–61.

Greenwald, A.G., Banaji, M.R., Rudman, L.A., Farnham, S.D., Nosek, B.A. & Mellott, D.S. (2002). A unified theory of implicit attitudes, stereotypes, self-esteem, and self-concept. *Psychological Review*, 109(1), 3–25.

Guerci, M., Radaelli, G. & Shani, A.B. (Rami) (2019). Conducting mode 2 research in HRM: A phase-based framework. *Human Resource Management*, 58, 5–20.

Hansen, A.V. & Madsen, S. (2019). *Theorizing in organization studies: Lessons from key thinkers.* Cheltenham, UK and Northampton, MA, USA: Edward Elgar Publishing.

Hatchuel, A. (2005). Towards an epistemology of collective action. *European Management Review*, 2(1), 36–47.

Hay, A. & Samra-Fredericks, D. (2019). Bringing the heart and soul back in: Collaborative inquiry and the DBA. *Academy of Management Learning & Education*, 18(1), 59–80.

Heifetz, R.A. & Heifetz, R. (1994). *Leadership without easy answers*. Boston, MA: Harvard University Press.

Heron, J. & Reason, P. (1997). A participatory inquiry paradigm. *Qualitative Inquiry*, 3, 274–94.

Heron, J. & Reason, P. (2008). Extending epistemology within a cooperative inquiry. In P. Reason & H. Bradbury (Eds.), *The Sage handbook of action research*, 2nd edn. (pp. 366–80). London: Sage.

Hibbert, P. & Huxham, C. (2005). A little about the mystery: Process learning as collaboration evolves. *European Management Review*, 2, 59–69.

Huxham, C. & Vangen, S. (2005). *Managing to collaborate*. New York: Routledge.

Janis, I.L. (1972). *Victims of groupthink*. Boston, MA: Houghton Mifflin.

Jones, J.C. (1970). *Design methods*. Chichester, UK: Wiley.

Jorgenson, J. & Steier, F. (2013). Frames, framing, and designed conversational processes: Lessons from the world café. *Journal of Applied Behavioral Science*, 49(3), 388–405.

Kaplan, A. (1964). *The conduct of inquiry*. New York: Crowell.

Kolb, D.A. (1984). *Experiential learning*. Englewood Cliffs, NJ: Prentice-Hall.

Kolodny, H., Stymne, B., Shani, A.B. (Rami), Figuera, J.R. & Lillrank, P. (2001). Design and policy choices for technology extension organizations. *Journal of Research Policy*, 30(1), 201–25.

Kotter, J.P (1996). *Leading change*. Boston, MA: Harvard Business School Press.

Kotter, J.P. & Cohen, D.S. (2002). *The heart of change*. Boston, MA: Harvard Business School Press.

Kraus, W.A. (1980). *Collaboration in organizations: Alternatives to hierarchy*. New York: Human Sciences Press.

Kupp, M., Anderson, J. & Reckhenrich, J. (2017). Why design thinking in business needs a rethink. *Sloan Management Review*, 59(1), 41–4.

Lawler, E.E. & Worley, C. (2011). *Management reset: Organizing for sustainable effectiveness*. San Francisco, CA: Jossey-Bass.

Lawson, B. (2006). *How designers think: The design process demystified*. New York: Elsevier.

Lillrank, P., Shani, A.B. (Rami) & Lindberg, P. (2001). Continuous improvement: Exploring alternative organizational designs. *Total Quality Management*, 12(1), 41–55.

Lipshitz, R., Friedman, V.J. & Popper, M. (2007). *Demystifying organizational learning*. Thousand Oaks, CA: Sage.

Lipshitz, R., Popper, M. & Oz, S. (1996). Building learning organizations: The design and implementation of organizational learning mechanisms. *Journal of Applied Behavioral Science*, 32, 292–305.

Livne-Tarandach, R. & Bartunek, J.M. (2009). A new horizon for organizational change and development scholarship: Connecting planned and emergent change. In R.W. Woodman, W.A. Pasmore & Abraham B. (Rami)

Shani (Eds.), *Research in organizational change and development* (Vol. 17, pp. 1–36). Greenwich, CT: JAI Press.

Lonergan, B.J. (1992). *The collected works of Bernard Lonergan, Vol 4 Insight: An essay in human understanding.* Toronto: Toronto University Press.

MacIntosh, R., Bartunek, J.M., Bhatt, M. & MacLean, D. (2016). I never promised you a rose garden: When research questions ought to change. In D.A. Noumair & A.B. (Rami) Shani (Eds.), *Research in organizational change and development* (Vol. 24, pp. 47–82). Bingley, UK: Emerald.

MacKenzie, K.D. (1986). *Organization design: The organization audit and analysis technology.* New York: Ablex.

MacLachlan, G., & Reid, I. (1994). *Framing and interpretation.* Melbourne, Vic.: Melbourne University Press.

MacLean, D. & MacIntosh, R. (2012). Strategic change as creative action. *Journal of Strategic Change Management*, 4(1), 80–97.

MacLean, D., MacIntosh, R. & Seidi, D. (2015). Rethinking dynamic capabilities from a creative action perspective. *Strategic Organization*, 13(4), 340–52.

March, J.G. (1991). Exploration and exploitation in organizational learning. *Organization Science*, 2, 71–87.

Martin, R. (2009). *The design of business.* Boston, MA: Harvard Business Review Press.

Mattessich, P.W. & Johnson, K.M. (2018). *Collaboration: What makes it work.* New York: Fieldstone Alliance.

Maxton, P.J. & Bushe, G.R. (2018). Individual cognitive effort and cognitive transition during organization development. *Journal of Applied Behavioral Science*, 54(4), 424–56.

McGrath, R. & McManus, R. (2020). Discovery-driven digital transformation. *Harvard Business Review*, 98(3), 124–33.

McGregor, D. (1960). *The human side of enterprise.* New York: McGraw Hill.

Miller, J.H. & Page, S.E. (2007). *Complex adaptive systems.* Princeton, NJ: Princeton University Press.

Mirvis, P.H. (2002). Community building in business. *Reflections: The SoL Journal*, 3(3), 46–52.

Mirvis, P.H. & Googins, B. (2006). Stages of corporate citizenship: A developmental framework. *California Management Review*, 48(2), 104–26.

Mirvis, P. H. & Marks, M.L. (2017). Co-researching and doing M&A integration: Crossing the scholar-practitioner divide. In A.B. (Rami) Shani & D.A. Noumair (Eds.), *Research in organizational change and development* (Vol. 25, pp. 171–202). Bingley, UK: Emerald.

Mitki, Y., Shani, A.B. (Rami), & Stjerberg, T. (2000). A typology of change programs. In R.T. Golembiewski (Ed.), *Handbook of organizational consultation* (pp. 777–85). New York: Dekker.

Mohrman, S.A., Lawler, E.E. III, & Associates (2011). *Useful research: Advancing theory and practice.* Oakland, CA: Berrett-Koehler.

Mohrman. S.A. & Pillans, G. (2013). *Emerging approaches to organization design.* London: Corporate Research Forum Publication.

Mohrman, S.A. & Shani, A.B. (Rami) (2008). The multiple voices of collaboration: A critical reflection. In A.B. (Rami) Shani, S. Mohrman, W.A. Pasmore,

B. Stymne & N. Adler (Eds.), *Handbook of collaborative management research*, (pp. 531–8). Thousand Oaks, CA: Sage.

Neilsen, E.H. (1984). *Becoming an OD practitioner.* Englewood Cliffs, NJ: Prentice-Hall.

Nickerson, R.S. (1998). Confirmation bias: A ubiquitous phenomenon in many guises. *Review of General Psychology*, 2(2), 175–220.

Nielsen, R. (2017). Who do we identify with? Ontological and epistemological challenges of spanning different domains of academic-practitioner praxis. In J.M. Bartunek and J. McKenzie (Eds.), *Academic practitioner research partnerships: Developments, complexities and opportunities* (pp. 50–64). Abingdon: Routledge.

Nonaka, I. & Konno, N. (1998). The concept of "ba": Building a foundation for knowledge creation. *California Management Review*, 40(3), 40–54.

Nonaka, I., Toyama, R. & Byosiere, P. (2001). A theory of organizational knowledge creation: Understanding the dynamic process of creating knowledge. In A. Antal, M. Dierkes, J. Child & I. Nonaka (Eds.), *Handbook of organizational learning and knowledge* (pp. 491–517). New York: Oxford University Press.

Norman, D.A. (2010). *Design thinking: A useful myth.* New York: Basic Books.

Nowotny, H., Scott, P. & Gibbons, M. (2001). *Re-thinking science: Knowledge and the public in an age of uncertainty.* Cambridge: Polity Press.

Nowotny, H., Scott, P. & Gibbons, M. (2003). 'Mode 2' revisited: The new production of knowledge. *Minerva*, 41, 179–94.

Palus, C.J. & Drath, W.H. (2001). *Understanding leadership development.* Greensborough, NC: Center for Creative Leadership Press.

Pasmore, W.A. (1988). *Designing effective organizations: The sociotechnical systems perspective.* New York: Wiley.

Pasmore, W.A. (2001). Action research in the workplace: The socio-technical perspective. In P. Reason & H. Bradbury (Eds.), *The handbook of action research* (pp. 38–47). London: Sage.

Pasmore, W.A. (2015). *Leading continuous change: Navigating change in the real world.* Oakland, CA: Berrett-Koehler.

Pasmore, W.A. (2020). *Advanced consulting: Earning trust at the highest level.* Oakland, CA: Berrett-Koehler.

Pasmore, W., Winby, S., Mohrman, S.A. & Vanasse, R. (2019). Reflections: Sociotechnical systems design and organization change. *Journal of Change Management*, 19(2), 67–85.

Pasmore, W.A., Woodman, R.W. & Simmons, A.L. (2008). Towards a more rigorous, reflective, and relevant science of collaborative management research. In A.B. (Rami) Shani, S.A. Mohrman, W.A. Pasmore, B. Stymne & N. Adler (Eds.), *Handbook of collaborative management research* (pp. 569–84). Thousand Oaks, CA: Sage.

Peck, M.S. (1987). *The different drum: Community making and peace.* New York: Simon and Schuster.

Peirce, C.S. (1903) [1997]. Pragmatism as a principle and method of right thinking. In P.A. Turrisi (Ed.), *The 1903 Harvard lectures on pragmatism.* Albany, NY: State University of New York Press.

Pendleton-Jullian, A.M. & Brown, S. (2018). *Design unbound: Designing for emergence in a whitewater world.* Boston, MA: MIT Press.

Popper, M. & Lipshitz, R. (1998). Organizational learning mechanisms: A structural and cultural approach to organizational learning. *Journal of Applied Behavioral Science,* 34(2), 161–79.

Porter, W.A. (1988). Notes on the logic of designing: Two thought-experiments. *Design Studies,* 9(3), 20–32.

Press, J., Bellis, P., Buganza, T., Maganini, S., Shani, A.B. (Rami), Trabucchi, D., Verganti, R. & Zasa, F.P. (2020). *Innovation and design as leadership: Transformation in the digital era.* Milan: IDeaLs.

Press, J., Verganti, R., Buganza, T. & Shani, A.B. (Rami) (2020). *Design-driven transformation: Leadership for innovation with impact.* Greensboro, NC: CCL Publications.

Rajagopalan, N. (2020). Rigor, relevance, and resilience in management research. *Journal of Management Inquiry,* 29(2), 150–53.

Ravasi, D. and Stigliani, I. (2012). Product design: A review and research agenda for management studies. *International Journal of Management Reviews,* 14(4), 464–88.

Reason, P. (Ed.) (1988). *Human inquiry in action: Developments in new paradigm research.* London: Sage.

Revans, R. (1998). *ABC of action learning.* London: Lemos & Crane.

Romanelli, E. & Tushman, M.L. (1994). Organizational transformation as punctuated equilibrium: An empirical test. *Academy of Management Journal,* 37(5), 1141–66.

Rittel, H.W. & Webber, M.M. (1973). Dilemmas in a general theory of planning. *Policy Sciences,* 4(2), 155–69.

Roth, J., Shani, A.B. (Rami) & Leary, M. (2008). Insider action research: The challenges of new capability development within a biopharma company. *Action Research,* 5(1), 41–60.

Ruggiero, V.C. (1999). *Becoming a critical thinker.* Boston, MA: Houghton Mifflin.

Schein, E.H. (1969). *Process consultation: Its role in organization development.* Reading, MA: Addison-Wesley.

Schein, E.H. (1987). *The clinical perspective in fieldwork.* Thousand Oaks, CA: Sage.

Schein, E.H. (1999). *Process consultation revisited: Building the helping relationship.* Reading, MA: Addison-Wesley.

Schein, E.H. (2009a). Reactions, reflections, rejoiners and a challenge. *Journal of Applied Behavioral Science,* 45(1), 141–58.

Schein, E.H. (2009b). *Helping: How to offer, give, and receive help.* Oakland, CA: Berrett-Koehler.

Schein, E.H. (2010). Organization development: Science, technology or philosophy? In D. Coghlan & A.B. (Rami) Shani (Eds.), *Fundamentals of organization development* (Vol. 1, pp. 91–100). London: Sage.

Schein, E.H. (2013). *Humble inquiry: The gentle art of asking instead of telling.* Oakland, CA: Berrett-Koehler.

Schein, E.H. (2016). *Humble consulting.* Oakland, CA: Berrett-Koehler.

Schein, E.H. & Schein, P.A. (2017). *Organizational culture and leadership*. 5th edn. San Francisco, CA: Jossey-Bass.
Schein. E.H. & Schein, P.A. (2019). *The corporate culture survival guide*. 3rd. edn. Hoboken, NJ: Wiley.
Schön, D. (1983). *The reflective practitioner*. New York: Basic Books.
Schön, D. (1988). Designing: rules, types and worlds. *Design Studies*, 9(3), 181–90.
Schön, D. A. and Rhein, M. (1994). *Frame reflection: Toward the resolution of intractable policy controversies*. New York: Basic Books.
Selsky, J.W. & Parker, B. (2010). Platforms for cross-sector social partnerships: Prospective sensemaking devices for social benefits. *Journal of Business Ethics*, 82, 233–50.
Senge, P. (1990). *The fifth discipline*. New York: Doubleday.
Shani, A.B. (Rami), Coghlan, D. & Alexander, B. (2020). Rediscovering abductive reasoning in organization development and change research. *Journal of Applied Behavioral Science*, 56(1), 60–72.
Shani, A.B. (Rami), Coghlan, D. & Cirella, S. (2012). Action research and collaborative management research: More than meets the eye? *International Journal of Action Research*, 8(1), 45–67.
Shani, A.B. (Rami) & Docherty, P. (2003), *Learning by design: Building sustainable organizations*. Oxford: Blackwell.
Shani A.B. (Rami) & Docherty, P. (2008). Learning by design: A fundamental foundation for organization development change programs. In T.G. Cummings (Ed.), *Handbook of organization development* (pp. 163–81). Thousand Oaks, CA: Sage.
Shani, A.B. (Rami) & Elliott, O. (1998). Applying sociotechnical system design at the strategic apex. *Organization Development Journal*, 6(2), 53–66.
Shani, A.B. (Rami), Greenbaum, B.E. & Verganti, R. (2018). Innovation through radical circles: Insights from organizational transformation of a middle school. *Organization Development Journal*, 36(2), 75–87.
Shani, A.B. (Rami), Mohrman, S., Pasmore, W.A., Stymne, B. & Adler, N. (Eds.) (2008). *Handbook of collaborative management research*. Thousand Oaks, CA: Sage.
Shani, A.B. (Rami) & Stebbins, M. (1987). Organization design: Emerging trends. *Consultation: An International Journal*, 6(5), 187–94.
Shani, A.B. (Rami), Tenkasi, R. & Alexander, B. (2017). Knowledge and practice: A historical perspective on collaborative management research. In J. Bartunek & J. McKenzie (Eds.), *Academic practitioner research partnership: Developments, complexities and opportunities* (pp. 17–34). Abingdon: Routledge.
Sharma, G. & Bansal, P. (2020). Cocreating rigorous and relevant knowledge. *Academy of Management Journal*, 63(2), 386–410.
Simon, H.A. (1996). *The sciences of the artificial*. Cambridge, MA: MIT Press.
Solari, L., Coghlan, D. & Shani A.B. (Rami) (2015). Sense making in collaborative management research: Insights from an Italian social cooperative. In A.B. (Rami) Shani & D.A. Noumair (Eds.), *Research in organizational change and development* (Vol. 23, pp. 167–94). Bingley, UK: Emerald.

Spreitzer, G.B., Acevice, P., Hendricks, H. & Garrett, L. (2020). Community in the world of work: Implications for organizational development and thriving. In D.A. Noumair & A.B. (Rami) Shani (Eds.), *Research in organizational change and development* (Vol. 28, pp. 77–101). Bingley, UK: Emerald.

Stebbins, M.W., Freed, T., Shani, A.B. (Rami) & Doerr, K. (2006). Reflection in the context of organizational secrecy. In D. Boud, P. Cressey & P. Docherty (Eds.), *Productive reflection and learning at work* (pp. 80–93). London: Routledge.

Stebbins, M. and Shani, A.B. (Rami) (1989a). Communication forum intervention: A longitudinal study. *Leadership & Organization Development Journal*, 4(5), 3–9.

Stebbins, M. & Shani, A.B. (Rami) (1989b). Moving away from the 'mafia' model of organization design. *Organizational Dynamics*, 17(3), 18–30.

Stebbins, M. & Shani, A.B. (Rami) (2009). Clinical inquiry and reflective design in a secrecy-based organization. *Journal of Applied Behavioral Sciences*, 45(1), 59–89.

Swedberg, R. (Ed.) (2014). *Theorizing in social science*. Stanford, CA: Stanford University Press.

Taylor, S. & Hansen, H. (2005). Finding form: Looking at the field of organizational aesthetics. *Journal of Management Studies*, 42(6), 1211–31.

Teece, D.J. (2007). Explicating dynamic capabilities and strategic management. *Strategic Management Journal*, 28, 1319–50.

Teece, D.J., Pisano, G. & Schuen, A. (1997). Dynamic capabilities and strategic management. *Strategic Management Journal*, 18(7), 509–30.

Thompson, G.J., Frances, R., Levacic, R. & Mitchell, J. (Eds.) (2009). *Markets, hierarchies and networks*. London: Sage.

Todnem By, R. (2005). Organizational change management: A critical review. *Journal of Change Management*, 5(4), 369–80.

Toulmin, S. (1990). *Cosmopolis: The hidden agenda of modernity*. Chicago, IL: University of Chicago Press.

Van de Ven, A.H. (2007). *Engaged scholarship*. New York: Oxford University Press.

Van de Ven, A.H. (2011). Reflections of research for theory and practice: From an engaged scholarship perspective. In S.A. Mohrman, E.E. Lawler & Associates (Eds.), *Useful research: Advancing theory and practice* (pp. 387–406). Oakland, CA: Berrett-Koehler.

Verganti, R. (2009). *Design driven innovation: Changing the rules of competition by radically innovating what things mean*. Boston, MA: Harvard Business Review Press.

Verganti, R. (2017). *Overcrowded: designing meaningful products in a world awash with ideas*. Boston, MA: MIT Press.

Verganti, R. & Shani, A.B. (Rami) (2016). Vision transformation through radical circles: Enhancing innovation capability development. *Organizational Dynamics*, 45, 104–13.

Weick, K.E. (1995). *Sensemaking in organizations*. Thousand Oaks, CA: Sage.

Weick, K.E. (1996). Drop your tools: An allegory for organizational studies. *Administrative Science Quarterly*, 41(2), 301–13.

Wenger, E. (1998). *Communities of practice: Learning, meaning, and identity.* Cambridge: Cambridge University Press.

Wischnevsky, J.D. & Damanpour, F. (2006). Organizational transformation and performance: An examination of three perspectives. *Journal of Managerial Issues*, 18, 104–28.

Woodman, R.W. (2014). The science of organizational change and the art of changing organizations. *Journal of Applied Behavioral Science*, 50, 463–77.

Worley, C.G. & Mirvis, P. (Eds.) (2013). *Building networks and partnerships.* Bingley, UK: Emerald.

Index

abductive reasoning 40–44, 91
Ackerman, A.L. 52, 53
action learning 48
action research 9, 22
Adler, N.J. 93
Anderson, D. 52, 53
Antal, A 18
appreciative inquiry 48
Argyris, C. 17, 18, 41, 44, 83, 100

Bailey, K.D. 49
Bansal, P. 103
Bartunek, J.M. 27, 28, 52, 53, 54,
    55, 62
Beckhard, R. 20
Beer, M. xiv–xvi, 1, 7, 20, 21, 24, 54,
    58, 60, 74, 75, 101
Bell, C. 20
Bellis, P. 28, 29, 62, 64
Bennis, W.G. 23
Bertalanffy, L. 4
Bohm, D. 24
Bradbury, H. 6, 49
Brown, J. 24
Brown, L.D. 23
Brown, S. 64
Brunelli, M. x–xiii
Bruner, J. S. 98
Bruning, R.H. 54
Buono, A. F. 53, 54
Burnes, B. 6, 20, 21, 22
Burns, T. 23
Bushe, G. R. 9, 19, 24, 28, 33, 54, 57,
    76, 81, 102

Cameron, K.S. xii
Campbell, D. 4
Canterino, F. 76
Checkland, P. 4

Cirella, S. 18
clinical inquiry 48
Coghlan, D. 5, 6, 7, 9, 17, 21, 22, 25,
    30, 31, 33, 38, 42, 43, 44, 46,
    48, 49, 50, 60, 68, 83, 86, 90,
    91, 93
Cohen, D.S. 54
Cohen, M.D. 17
collaboration, 26–8
collaborative inquiry
    definition 2–3
    design and designers 59–66
    ethical challenges 49–50
    key elements 3–5
    methodology and methods
        36–51, 93
    modalities 48–9
    phases and mechanisms 68–80
    process 44–8
    quality 80–85
    researchers 90–91
    skills 90–91
    theoretical foundations 17–35,
        26–31
    theorizing 89–91
    transformational change 52–9
Collatto, D. 28
Conklin, J. 98
Cooke, B. 6, 20, 21, 22
Cooperrider, D. 49
Coughlan, P. 5, 17, 60
Cronin, B. 38
Cross, R. 28
Csikzentmihalyi, M. 98
Cummings, T.G. 20

Dananpour, F. 55
de Geus, A. 17
Delbecq, A. 93

design perspective 59–66
design science 29
dialogic organization development 9
Dialogue 24–5
Dixon, N.M. 19, 81
Docherty, P. 17, 19, 28, 74, 81
Drath, W.H. 24, 30
Dresch, A. 28

Elliott, O. 57
Emery, F. 4
engaged scholarship 8, 86
ethical challenges 49–50
extended epistemology 8

Fredberg, T. 58
Freeman, R. E. 25
French, W. L. 20
Friedlander, F. 21
Friedman, V. 8, 18, 19, 25, 27

Gagliardi, P. 100
Galbraith, J.R. 54, 60
Galuppo, L. 25
Garvin, D.A. 17
general empirical method 42–44, 45,
    47–8
generativity 28–30
Gergen, K.J. 25
Gibbons, M.1, 2, 30–31
Goggins, B. 25
Grant, R.M. 11
Gray, B. 25, 27
Greenbaum, B. 53, 55, 59
Greenwald, A. G. 100
Guerci, M. 68

Hansen, A.V. 91
Hansen, H. 100
Hatchuel, A. 62
Hay, A. 26
Heifetz, R. A. 98
Heron, J. 8, 33, 48, 87
Hibbert, P. 27
human knowing 38–40
Humble inquiry 8
Huxham, C. 7, 27

innovation of meaning 29
inquiring in the present tense 31–2
inquiry modes 45
interiority 87–9
interpretive schemas 28

Janis, I. L. 100
Johnson. K.M. 26
Jones, E.B. 52, 54, 55
Jones, J.C. 62
Jorgenson, J. 54, 62

Kaplan, A. 49
Kerber, K.W. 53, 54
knowledge creation 7–10, 86–91
Kolb, D. A. 17, 87
Kolodny, H. 65
Konno, N. 19, 101
Kotter, J.P. 54
Kraus, W.A. 6
Kupp, M. 62

Lawler, E.E. 54
Lawson, B. 62
learning history 49
learning mechanisms 19–20
Lillrank, P. 64
Lipshitz, R. 5, 17, 19, 81
Livne-Tarandach, R. 53, 54
Lonergan, B.J. 38
Louis, M.R. 62

MacIntosh, R. 76, 77, 78, 92
MacKenzie, K.D. 60
MacLachlan, G. 80
MacLean, D. 78
Mainmelis, C. 49
March, J.G. 5, 17
Marks, M. L. 194
Marshak, R. 9, 24, 28, 33, 76, 102
Martin, R. 62
Mattessich, P.W. 26
Maxton, P.J. 54
McGrath, R. 1
McGregor, D. xiv
McManus, R. 1
Miller, J.H. 4

Mirvis, P. H. 25, 102, 103, 104
Mitki, Y. 52
Mode 1 knowledge production 2, 103, 32
Mode 2 knowledge production 1–2, 30–31, 32
Mohrman, S.A. 7, 11, 27, 31, 60, 68

Nickerson, R. S. 100
Neilsen, E.H. 6
Nielsen, R. 50
Nishada, K. 19
Nonaka, I. 19–20, 101

olive tree metaphor 95–7
organization development and change 20–26
organization transformation 50–59
organizations as complex adaptive systems 4–6
organizations as learning systems 17–20
organizations as social constructions 4

Page, S.E. 4
Palus, C.J. 24, 30
Parker, B. 25
Partnership, 6, 25–6
Pasmore, W.A. 1, 6, 54, 55, 60, 67, 182–5
Peck, M. S. 101
Peirce, C.S. 40–41
Pendleton-Jullian, A.M. 64
Pillans, G. 60
Popper, M. 19
Porter, W.A. 63
practical knowing 33–5, 87
Press, J. 28, 29, 60, 62, 64
process consultation, 8

Quinn, R.E. xii

Rajagopalan, N. 67, 82–3
Ravasi, D. 30
Reason, P. 8, 48, 68, 87
Reid, I 80

Revans, R. 48
Rittel, H. 98
Romanelli, E. 55
Roth, J. 64
Ruggiero, V.C. 98
Rynes, S.L. 27

Samra-Fredricks, D. 26
Schein, E.H. 6, 7, 8, 29, 20, 21, 22, 41, 42, 44–5, 48, 91, 103
Schein, P.A. 19, 41, 91
Schon, D.A. 17, 18, 62, 64
Selsky, J.W. 25
Senge, P. 17
Shani, A.B. (Rami) 7, 9, 17, 19, 23, 25, 26, 27, 28, 31, 55, 58, 59, 60, 68, 74, 81, 86, 91
Sharma, G. 103
Simon, H.A. 29, 62
social space 31
Solari, L. 29
Spreitzer, G. B. 1
Sproull, L.S. 17
Stalker, G.M. 23
Stebbins, M.W. 57, 60, 66
Steier, F. 54, 62
Stigliani, I. 30
Swedberg, R. 91

Taylor, S. 100
Teece, D.J. 11
Thompson, G.J. 27
Todnem By, R. (2005) 54, 55
Toulmin, S. 33
Trist, E. 4
transformational change 52–9
Tushman, M. 55

Van de Ven, A. H. 8, 31, 68, 86
Vangen, S. 7
Verganti, R. 1, 29, 59, 60, 62
VUCA, 1

ways of knowing 8, 32–3
Webber, M.M. 98
Weick, K.E. 30. 101
Wenger, E. 29

Wischnevsky, J.D. 55

Woodman, R.W. 22, 36, 89

Worley, C. G. 54, 103